CEO
POTENTIAL

CEO
POTENTIAL

TRANSCEND SELF, TEAM, AND
ORGANIZATION FOR LASTING
SUCCESS IN THE NEW AGE OF AI

DAVE OSH

Hardback ISBN: 979-8-9915595-0-8

Paperback ISBN: 979-8-9915595-1-5

eBook ISBN: 979-8-9915595-2-2

Audio ISBN: 979-8-9915595-3-9

Library of Congress Control Number: 2024922304

Copyright Office Number 1-14357214521

"More than a leadership manual—it's a blueprint for transformation. Osh provides a clear path for CEOs to cultivate deeper self-awareness and organizational impact."

- Rick Wilmer, CEO, ChargePoint

"Dave Osh captures and redefines what it means to be a CEO in today's world—by focusing on Potential as an ever-evolving capacity and source of growth. It's refreshing, insightful, and game-changing for those leaders looking further and deeper than just a few quarters."

- Rob Castaneda, CEO, ServiceRocket

"In CEO Potential, Dave Osh distills the essence of leadership development, presenting a clear and actionable framework for unlocking the full potential of leaders in an ever-evolving business landscape. This book is the strategic upgrade every CEO needs to not only survive but thrive in the complexity of modern business

– Ron Scheese, CEO, Andesa Services

"As a CEO, I found this book to be an invaluable resource for today's leaders. In the challenging age of AI, Dave Osh delivers an encouraging message: leadership potential is not fixed but can grow for those who seek it. The book's engaging narrative, following a fictional CEO's journey, makes complex ideas easy to grasp. Osh skillfully turns adult development theories into actionable strategies, with self-assessments, case studies, and real-world examples to help leaders customize their growth journey. Get ready to unlock new levels of potential!"

- Brian Underhill, CEO, CoachSource

"A brilliant blend of developmental psychology and practical leadership insights. This book doesn't just show you what's possible; it shows you how to get there."

- Arman Eshraghi, CEO, Qrvey

"A compelling journey into the untapped power of leadership development. *CEO Potential* is an eye-opener for any leader committed to long-term, transformative change."

- Bruno Larvol, CEO, Larvol

"Dave Osh not only believes in your potential to grow as a leader and CEO but takes a groundbreaking approach to showing how you can increase your potential through actionable, practical stories, research, and advice. This book will inspire you to level up for your team and show you how you can do it. "

- Scott Francis, CEO, BP3 Global

Dave's book brings much-needed clarity, offering actionable strategies for building high-performance teams and driving transformative leadership. It's a must-read for CEOs dedicated to fostering a strong organizational culture and enhancing stakeholder value."

- André V. Chapman, CEO Emeritus, Unity Care

"'CEO Potential' cuts through the noise, providing a clear and compelling framework to evolve leadership. A rare gem that truly connects theory with actionable practice."

- Zeina El-Azzi, CEO, Gage Zero

"This book will help any CEO unlock new levels of awareness, agility, and effectiveness in leadership, blending practical wisdom with profound insights."

- Kunal Chopra, Chairman, Aventis Alpha Care

"Dave Osh offers a holistic approach to leadership development that's both eye-opening and transformative. An invaluable guide to navigating today's complex business world. "

- Tom Salonek, CEO of Intertech

"A transformative guide for leaders seeking to break through their limitations and elevate their effectiveness and impact. A must-read for a CEO committed to growth."

- Yuval Lirov, CEO, ClinicMind

Dedicated to my beloved clients who navigate with me on the lifelong journey of leadership transcendence.

CONTENTS

PART 1

POTENTIAL FRAMEWORK

CHAPTER 1

REDEFINING POTENTIAL

At this very moment, someone is talking about you. It could be your boss, a colleague, or a customer. Perhaps it's your spouse, your child, or a parent. Someone, somewhere, is speaking about you behind your back—and they're all wrong. They believe they know who you are, that you're set in stone, unchangeable. It's just "your personality," they say.

We are going to prove them wrong.

The idea that "we are who we are" is a pervasive myth that has deeply influenced our lives, families, communities, and society. You've probably taken a personality test, looking for insights on how to communicate, collaborate, and tolerate different personalities. Not long ago, we believed that our brains stopped developing in our mid-twenties. However, neuroscientists studying neuroplasticity have thoroughly debunked this belief.

These scientists have shown that our minds can continue to develop throughout our lives. This understanding led psychologists to create adult development theories, which have been widely applied in leadership development.

Through these scientific breakthroughs, we now know that what we often call 'personality' isn't fixed. It's just a stage in our ongoing development—a stage I refer to as "Potential." In this book, Potential isn't just a theoretical concept; it's your capacity to lead with growing effectiveness. Just as we once saw personality traits as unchangeable, we now recognize behaviors as expressions of Potential. By changing our behaviors, we can transform our Potential, leading others to see us as having 'changed' our personalities.

The notion of 'full Potential' has also been overturned. Our brain's ability to form new neural pathways means we can continuously push beyond what we once considered our limits. This was emphasized by Anders Ericsson, a Professor of Psychology and author of *Peak*. His work, which inspired Malcolm Gladwell's *Outliers*, provided a foundational understanding: "The brain is far more adaptable than anyone ever imagined. Thinking of people as born with fixed Potential no longer makes sense. Potential is an expandable vessel."

This book aims to do more than debunk myths. It's designed to help you understand the various stages of Potential. You will identify your current stage, learn how to advance to the next level, and continue growing. This journey isn't just possible—it's within your reach.

The CEO Conundrum

Ari is the CEO of a tech company with 1,000 employees in the bustling San Francisco Bay Area. In his late forties and married, Ari is also a father to three teenagers on the brink of college.

He is constantly stressed about the future of his company. Debates with his executive team weigh heavily on him, making him feel as if the entire burden of the business is on his shoulders. At home, his relationships mirror his professional struggles. He finds it hard to connect with his wife and increasingly rebellious teenagers, and his attempts to maintain parental authority seem futile.

Ari's days are filled with lengthy discussions on business strategies, while his evenings are consumed by parenting debates with his wife. Mid-life burnout feels inevitable as he struggles with little success on multiple fronts. Two questions haunt him daily: "What's going on?" and "How can I fix this?"

Despite the chaos, Ari remains hopeful. He believes in a better version of himself that can set things right, though he hasn't figured out how to unlock this Potential.

As his company grows, its complexity increases. Rapid technological changes bring both opportunities and threats. At the same time, his personal life becomes more complicated. As his children navigate adolescence, their unpredictable behaviors challenge Ari and his wife's coping strategies.

Ari longs for simpler times when clear solutions exist for most problems. Now, he finds the landscape overwhelming, with countless approaches to each issue. While he believes he knows the way forward at work and home, aligning everyone with his vision remains difficult.

Increasingly, Ari relies on his authority more than he'd like, leading to feelings of inadequacy as both a leader and a parent. He recognizes that people resist decisions imposed without consensus and regrets his impatience in discussions.

No longer wanting to be the smartest person in the room, Ari is frustrated when stress drives him to revert to old, inauthentic behaviors that contradict his values.

At work, Ari deals with opinionated executives; at home, he faces stubborn family members. Both realms demand his attention, but he struggles to excel in either. Although Ari has charisma and influence, his patience often wears thin, leading him to assert unilateral power. Each time, he feels regret and believes he has failed as both a leader and a parent. In these moments, he confronts the limits of his current Potential.

The CEO Transformation

Fast forward 18 months, and everyone interacting with Ari—at work and at home—believes he has developed a 'new personality.' The truth is, he hasn't changed who he is; he has upgraded the 'operating system' that governs his behavior. He now views situations from perspectives that were once out of reach.

Today, Ari processes complex ideas with ease, drawing from diverse and often intangible sources. He reconciles conflicting viewpoints and integrates various systems and strategies effortlessly. Energized by his purpose, vision, and values, he revels in his newfound courage and authenticity. His leadership, now aligned with his values, greatly enhances his self-worth.

Ari has transformed his communication abilities. He engages in genuine dialogues with peers and family members—conversations that were impossible 18 months ago. He now gives and receives feedback effectively, offering critiques without putting others on the defensive and considering advice he previously ignored.

Conflicts, resentment, and resistance dissolve around him. People commit firmly to decisions, allowing him to hold them accountable without coercion. His visionary capabilities foster new collaborations, reducing the need for him to impose his views.

His teenagers appreciate the changes in him. They approach him openly, feeling heard, valued, and respected, even when they disagree. His empathetic listening has revitalized his marriage, offering a fresh start to a relationship that was once in decline.

Ari has created an environment where people at work and at home speak freely and act authentically. This deep connection with his team, board, and loved ones reveals an expansive new capacity to achieve more. He feels fulfilled and rewarded, having evolved into a better version of himself.

Write Your Transformation Story

If Ari's story resonates with you, you're not alone. If it inspires you, you're exactly where you need to be. Transcending your current Potential can have a lifelong impact.

This book will guide you in transforming your consciousness, effectiveness, and performance. I'll introduce you to the seven levels of Potential and explain how each level impacts your effectiveness and performance. Using this framework, you'll identify your current Potential and learn how to elevate it for yourself, your team, and your organization.

Leaders often feel overwhelmed by the many personal, team, and organizational development frameworks available. A unified framework promotes consistency and harmony.

Do you often feel lost or struggle to piece things together as they constantly shift? Enhancing your Potential aligns opposing forces and resolves conflicts in complex strategic decisions without relying on unilateral power.

The framework in this book has helped my clients—CEOs, executives, and their teams—become extraordinarily effective amidst hyper-complexity.

Walk in the Park

I thought my promotion to CEO would be a walk in the park. With a dose of arrogance, I believed I could handle the job effortlessly, even with both hands tied behind my back.

I was profoundly wrong.

After three years as COO, a lengthy board deliberation promoted me to CEO. I had already taken on many CEO duties—so what could one letter in my title change?

The difference was monumental. I had underestimated the shift when all my former peers began reporting to me. I hadn't anticipated the complexity of managing twelve board members, each with their own vision of what kind of CEO I should be.

If navigating these new professional waters wasn't challenging enough, unforeseen problems began to surface. It seemed like everyone was against me—the executive team, the board, business partners, and even the economy, as we entered the 2008 Great Recession. Misconceptions about my compensation caused unrest among my team, while rumors of layoffs destabilized the organization.

I blamed everyone for their apparent lack of support. My wife grew weary of my constant complaints. It never occurred to me that I might be the problem. I had reached the limits of my Potential, though I was unaware of it then.

The role was both familiar and utterly different. The multi-layered relationships were more complex and crucially more important than I had realized.

I had not yet evolved my consciousness to the level required for a CEO of a multinational company.

Three months into my tenure, I hit rock bottom despite reasonable business growth and promising new product lines. My leadership team, composed of my former peers, demanded a heart-to-heart conversation. They were blunt: "Dave, we are fed up because you aren't listening to us."

Their feedback mirrored that of my wife, Ainsley, who said, "Dave, I don't feel heard." Given that Ainsley avoids confrontation and my team does not, their aligned complaints were a clear signal that I needed to listen—and act.

I realized my issue wasn't just about performance. I had behaved like a general, failing to collaborate across the company's ecosystems.

The turning point came when I finally took ownership and decided to change. I began to observe, reflect, and act based on those reflections. Progress was slow and painful. I didn't have a coach or know the most effective ways to alter my behaviors. I was blind to the underlying fears, mindsets, assumptions, and belief systems driving those behaviors.

It took another five years to make substantial changes—still far from what was expected of a global leader. Only years later did the pieces of my leadership puzzle begin to fall into place after I learned about developmental models and underwent developmental 360° assessments. I wished I had known about the faster, more effective path to growth earlier.

I realized that my challenging first year as CEO stemmed from a subconscious need to prove my worth. This need drove me to push myself and others excessively hard. Here's a quick illustration:

During my first annual convention as CEO, I revamped the marketing team's presentation for a product launch, aiming for the most impressive debut ever. I modeled my presentation after Steve Jobs' iconic iPhone launch—not original, but effective. The event was a "success," and I basked in the recognition I craved.

However, months later, quality issues emerged. Responsibility slipped through the cracks because it was "Dave's product." My controlling tendencies had strained team relationships, and the product ultimately failed.

My fear of inadequacy led to assumptions and beliefs that hindered true leadership. Despite my reputation as 'Dave the Brave,' earned from years as a fighter pilot, my inflated ego, both from my military career and corporate roles, did not serve me well in thoughtful leadership.

After a diverse career across various countries and sectors, I continue to piece together leadership lessons from my past. The Leadership Potential Indicator assessment revealed I was only midway through the Potential continuum. This humbling insight has driven me to dedicate my life to reaching what I call Unitive Potential and helping other leaders accelerate their transformation.

This book is not just about personal growth; it aims to create a ripple effect of unity in a divided world by expanding leadership Potential. The framework you are about to learn transcends individual, team, organizational, and societal levels.

I've documented transformative changes and high performance in teams and executives. I've coached at companies like eBay, Netflix, Airbnb, Marvell, 10XGenomics, Stripe, FICO, Bill, Intuit, Udemy and Dolby, among others. This book shares the impact of this work on thousands of leaders worldwide, demonstrating the profound effects of expanded leadership Potential.

Let's Get Started

Now that we've set the stage, it's time to dive into transcending your Potential. I offer my unconditional commitment to your growth, avoiding the usual clichés found in 'transformation' books.

But before we proceed, I need your commitment. Are you ready to do whatever it takes to transcend your Potential? True transformation demands dedication and accountability. This journey is not for the faint of heart—it's a life-long path.

This book supports your growth, one Potential level at a time. The development process spans years, making this book more than a one-time read—it's a lifelong guide. Let's get started. Together, we'll explore the depths of your Potential and transform your effectiveness and impact.

CHAPTER 2.

LEVELS OF POTENTIAL

Standing on the Shoulders of Giants

In recent decades, developmental psychologists have made significant breakthroughs. They have identified seven levels of Potential we can reach. Typically, we operate from one default level.

These experts have developed assessments to determine the level of Potential individuals operate at. The results from thousands of these assessments are revealing—and somewhat disturbing. Only 15% of leaders operate at highly effective levels of Potential, while a staggering 85% function at less effective or outright ineffective levels. Alarmingly, just 5% have reached the most effective Potential available.

These findings are consistent across the board despite the psychologists working independently and using different scientific frameworks.

After years of collaborating with these scientists and helping leadership teams elevate their Potential using these models, I have synthesized the prominent frameworks into a unified, straightforward, and practical Potential development framework.

The acknowledgments section at the end of this book includes a complete list of my teachers, mentors, and coaches who have supported me and my clients' development. This section also compares the Potential levels described in this book with other development frameworks commonly used in business contexts.

What is Potential?

The phrase "realizing our full Potential" is overused. But what happens after we reach what we call our "full Potential"? Can we extend it even further? Absolutely! This is where things get exciting as we open ourselves to new possibilities, choices, and freedoms that our current level of Potential doesn't offer.

This book defines Potential as the capacity to handle complexity effectively. We can develop this ability through seven distinct stages.

Unlike biological growth, which happens naturally, developing our Potential requires intentional effort—it doesn't happen on its own. Many of us stay at the same level of Potential for decades or even our whole lives, held back by hidden ropes and anchors that keep us stuck in our current state.

As you read this book, you will uncover what is holding back your Potential and learn how to overcome these barriers. You'll find strategies to move to the next level of Potential. Investing in your Potential is often overlooked but offers the highest returns for your life and those around you—your family, team, and organization.

Let's dive into these seven levels of Potential.

Seven Levels of Potential

The seven levels of Potential show increasing degrees of self-awareness, each with a stronger ability to understand complex ideas and situations. These levels also represent different ways of thinking, feeling, and behaving—often mistaken for fixed personality traits.

As we progress through these levels, our worldview evolves. We move from seeing things in simple terms to grasping complexity, from static to dynamic perspectives, and from black-and-white thinking to recognizing a spectrum of colors and shades of grey.

Progressing through each level enhances our effectiveness and our ability to tackle the world's challenges. However, the greatest reward of advancing in Potential is the increased autonomy, freedom, and choice we experience. I coached leaders who have deepened their connections and discovered greater wisdom, fulfillment, and meaning.

We divide the seven levels of Potential into two main tiers: Centric and Transformer Potentials, similar to different operating systems. Centric Potential, the less effective tier, is like Potential 1.0. In contrast, Transformer Potential, the more effective tier, is akin to Potential 2.0.

Centric Potentials

About 85% of the leaders we assessed operate within four Centric Potentials: Self, Group, Domain, and Vision-Centric. These levels represent various versions of the Potential 1.0 operating system.

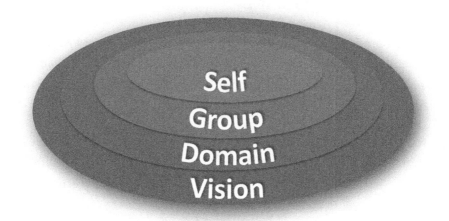

Figure 2.1 - Centric Potentials

All four Centric Potentials share a common trait: they are influenced by our cultural conditioning. We adjust our values and behaviors to align with our environment's expectations, structures, and power dynamics. Vision-Centric Potential is often idealized and praised in corporate settings, and many leadership books emphasize reaching this level. Companies often promote leaders to senior positions as they start to show Vision-Centric traits, sometimes too early, which places them under significant pressure to meet increased expectations.

Transformer Potentials

Only about 15% of the leaders we evaluated operate from Transformer Potential. These leaders have transcended their cultural conditioning and default values to create their own unique cultures. Operating from the Transformer levels—Expansive, Integral, and Unitive—these leaders adopt much broader perspectives. These levels represent various versions of the Potential 2.0 operating system.

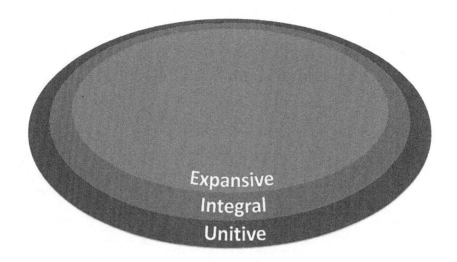

Figure 2.2 - Transformer Potentials

Each level of Potential integrates the previous ones. When you ascend to a higher level, the previous level remains a part of your repertoire, even as you primarily function from a more evolved state. This hierarchical integration explains some significant challenges in leadership teams, where Transformer leaders can easily understand Centric leaders, but Centric leaders often struggle to relate to Transformer leaders, leading to communication gaps and team dysfunction.

A CEO operating at the Vision-Centric level might struggle to lead individuals at the Expansive or Integral Transformer levels. This can hinder the growth of more advanced leaders.

Understanding the seven levels of Potential provides a clear roadmap for our development journey. It helps us navigate and improve our leadership skills more effectively.

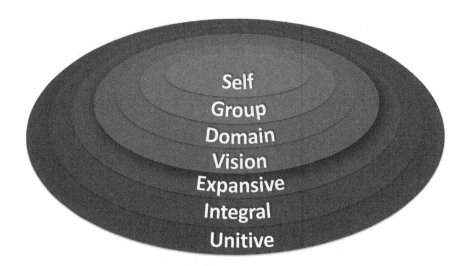

Figure 2.3 - Seven Levels of Potentials

Potential and Complexity

The more advanced our Potential, the better we can navigate complex environments. Leaders with higher levels of Potential are more adept at managing uncertainty and can adjust their behaviors in real time to keep pace with rapidly changing situations. On the other hand, leaders with less developed Potential often find such environments challenging.

Think of complex challenges as similar to difficult math problems with more variables than equations. These problems involve many interdependent factors that must be managed at once. For instance, a software provider selling products to streaming media companies faces a nuanced issue. If their product boosts subscriber numbers for some media companies but not for others, predicting the overall impact becomes complex due to the market players' interdependencies.

The more complex the situation, the more crucial Transformer Potentials become. If your work and life are straightforward, your current Potential may be adequate. But if you encounter intricate challenges, enhancing your Potential can greatly improve your effectiveness and performance.

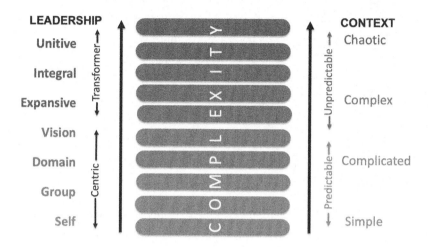

Figure 2.4 - Potential and Complexity

For example, if you head the payroll department in a large company, operating at the Group or Domain-Centric Potential might be sufficient. You can depend on established best practices since employment contracts and tax regulations are fairly stable. Frequent changes due to a manager's 'creativity' would be problematic.

However, a Chief Marketing Officer at a global company who operates solely at the Group or Domain-Centric Potential is likely to face difficulties over time. The complexities and shifting dynamics of global markets require a higher level of Potential to handle diverse and rapidly changing challenges effectively.

It's crucial to understand that Transformer Potentials aren't necessarily 'better' than Centric Potentials; they are simply more appropriate for different contexts. Centric Potentials work well when life and work are straightforward and don't require high adaptability.

As you explore the traits, strengths, and limitations of these levels, think about what Potential you and those around you might possess. Reflect on past experiences where you may have operated at each of the Centric Potentials. This self-examination will help you grasp why these levels vary so much and how they can be leveraged to meet your needs.

Self-Centric

It's rare to find individuals at the Self-Centric Potential within leadership teams. However, such individuals may inherit businesses or rise to high positions, like country presidents.

People at the Self-Centric level are primarily self-focused, showing minimal concern for others. They tend to be distrustful self-serving and can display manipulative or narcissistic tendencies. They often view relationships as opportunities for personal gain, seeing others as rivals or mere tools.

Leaders operating at this level might push legal and ethical boundaries, taking risks if they believe they can avoid consequences. They rationalize their behavior as acceptable and typically show no remorse. Feedback given to someone at the Self-Centric level is often rejected outright; they may blame the messenger and seek revenge. Retaliation is their usual approach, and they can go to great lengths to settle scores.

Such individuals are frequently perceived as bullies in the workplace, skilled in intellectual intimidation. Without advancing to a higher Potential level, their leadership is unlikely to be sustainable unless they own the business.

Those at the Self-Centric level may see themselves as superior, but their colleagues often do not share this view and find themselves constantly managing the fallout from the Self-Centric individual's rule-breaking.

Some organizations tolerate Self-Centric individuals because they are seen as risk-takers who can bring excitement and sometimes unexpected opportunities to the table.

At some point, most of us operated at the Self-Centric Potential, usually outgrowing it during adolescence as we learned to function within teams and group activities that required cooperation.

However, a few individuals remain stuck at this Potential into adulthood. Without intervention, it is exceedingly difficult for them to progress beyond this stage.

Group-Centric

Individuals functioning at the Group-Centric Potential generally display more kindness than those at the Self-Centric level. They show strong loyalty to their group and tend to adhere closely to collective norms, steering clear of actions that might go against the group's consensus.

A key characteristic of Group-Centric leaders is their tendency to please others, particularly their bosses and senior leaders. They are conflict-averse, seeking to avoid disagreements both in the workplace and at home. They work diligently to control their behavior, believing conformity to group norms will earn them acceptance and likability.

Group-Centric leaders play a vital role in creating harmony within teams. They act as the communal glue, attentive to the wants and needs of their colleagues, fostering a cooperative environment.

Individuals with Group-Centric Potential are often found in support roles like customer service, hospitality, or nursing. They might move into leadership positions over time, especially due to their experience and tenure. In these roles, they are often the most passive members of the leadership team. Their hesitation to voice dissent or challenge the status quo can make them appear as less assertive leaders.

These individuals are generally friendly and courteous but may struggle with delivering tough feedback to colleagues, direct reports, and even family members. Their reluctance to embrace innovation or drive change is often rooted in a fear of conflict or negative consequences, which contributes to a more conservative and cautious leadership style.

Most of us have experienced Group-Centric Potential during our college years and early careers as we tried to fit into professional environments and adapt to company cultures. Those who remain at this level as their careers advance may find it challenging to move up to the next stage of Potential, known as Domain-Centric.

Domain-Centric

The Domain-Centric level is common among company leaders. These individuals have built their identities on a foundation of knowledge and expertise, positioning themselves as the experts. The transition from Group to Domain-Centric typically occurs in our early career, as we gain domain expertise and move from conforming to others to establishing ourselves as authoritative experts.

Individuals operating at the Domain-Centric level are frequently perceived as highly controlling by those around them, including their children. When I shared my developmental assessment with my own kids, which highlighted high levels of control, they couldn't help but joke, "Dad, did you really need an assessment to confirm you're a control freak?"

Those at the Domain-Centric level find comfort in their expertise and often rely heavily on data to back up their views. They use this data to validate their opinions and persuade others of their correctness. Their perspective is often seen as the sole logical viewpoint, leading them to overlook alternative opinions and insights.

Efficiency is the core operating principle for Domain-Centric leaders. Commonly described as perpetually busy, they excel at creating new process improvements and striving for perfection in their fields. While these traits make them exceptional individual contributors, they can be problematic in leadership roles. If you report to a Domain-Centric leader, you might find that your efforts are never quite good enough. They tend to micromanage, driven by their perfectionist tendencies.

Colleagues frequently view Domain-Centric managers as arrogant and excessively critical. These managers often lead with a rigid, 'my-way-or-the-highway' mentality. While this approach can be effective in straightforward situations, it struggles in more complex scenarios.

For Domain-Centric leaders, collaboration seems unnecessary, and they generally dismiss the perspectives of their colleagues. They are likely to be irritated by invitations to workshops on topics like Emotional Intelligence, which they regard as irrelevant.

The greatest challenge for individuals at the Domain-Centric level is their difficulty in recognizing and appreciating diverse perspectives. This limitation acts as a major obstacle to their growth. To advance to the Vision-Centric Potential, they must let go of their need for control and the certainty of being right. Embracing alternative viewpoints is crucial for their development.

Vision-Centric

The Vision-Centric Potential is widely coveted and often highlighted in leadership, management, and business literature. Leaders at this level have a robust internal compass, or 'north star,' that directs their actions. They forge their identities from within and are less swayed by external opinions. Rather than strictly following best practices, they pioneer "next" practices that push boundaries and drive progress.

Vision-Centric leaders excel at integrating multiple perspectives, which fosters effective teamwork while simultaneously pushing and supporting their teams. They are adept at formulating inspiring visions and setting strategic goals to achieve them.

However, their strong focus on goals, outcomes, and deliverables can also be a drawback. This intense focus can sometimes become a limiting framework, constraining their ability to think outside established norms.

Generally, people find working for Vision-Centric leaders fulfilling. These leaders possess a nuanced understanding of complex issues and handle uncertainty and ambiguity with skill. They are open to feedback that aligns with their vision but may dismiss feedback that doesn't.

Vision-Centric leaders balance task orientation with relationship-building, believing that innovation is best achieved through collaboration. They communicate with courageous authenticity and vulnerability, guided by a deep sense of purpose and integrity.

They embrace conflict as a natural part of progress, understanding that differing opinions can lead to growth. Their ability to maintain relationship quality allows them to positively influence others without the need for control, conformity, or insisting on being right.

Vision-Centric leaders are well-suited for middle management roles, where they can implement new strategies and juggle both short- and long-term goals.

Despite their effectiveness, Vision-Centric leaders often face friction with Domain-Centric peers and direct reports, who may find their open-minded approach disruptive but acknowledge their success. This success can drive Domain-Centric leaders to aspire to Vision-Centric Potential. Organizations frequently advance Vision-Centric leaders more quickly than their Domain-Centric counterparts.

Transitioning from Domain-Centric to Vision-Centric can be challenging because Domain-Centric leaders often believe their expertise is the cornerstone of their success. Letting go of what has worked for them can be especially difficult for those later in their careers.

However, if Vision-Centric Potential is so effective, why strive to go beyond it? While sufficient for many roles and industries, Vision-Centric leaders working in highly unpredictable and complex environments—such as leading multinational teams or navigating rapidly evolving technologies—will encounter limitations. This is where advancing to Transformer Potential becomes crucial.

Transformer Potentials, though less explored, present new challenges and opportunities. So, prepare to explore this uncharted territory as we dive into what lies beyond the Vision-Centric Potential.

Expansive Transformer

The Expansive Transformer Potential acts as a crucial bridge leading to the Integral Transformer Potential. At this stage, leaders start to question their own mindsets, beliefs, and assumptions, evolving toward a more comprehensive understanding of their world.

Leaders at the Expansive Transformer level assess the alignment between their core values and their actual behaviors, setting them apart from those operating at the Vision-Centric level. They are highly aware of the discrepancies between their principles and their actions or between their statements and their conduct. This heightened awareness stimulates their creativity and drives personal growth as they work to reconcile these inconsistencies.

As Expansive Transformers confront and address the gaps between their ideals and their behaviors, they begin to move beyond the constraints of their previous cultural conditioning. This phase often leads to notable breakthroughs but can also create friction with others who may perceive their actions as unconventional or irrational. While some may view them as unpredictable or wild cards, others appreciate their political acumen and their ability to achieve ambitious goals despite encountering resistance and pushback.

One of the greatest challenges for leaders transitioning into the Expansive Transformer Potential is managing relationships with colleagues who operate at the Vision and Domain-Centric levels. These colleagues may struggle to understand the unconventional strategies and broader insights of an Expansive Transformer.

For example, if you are an Expansive CEO, you have the capacity to exemplify transformational behavior that others can emulate. However, if you are an Expansive leader working for a CEO who operates from a Vision-Centric or Domain-Centric perspective, you may encounter significant hurdles. These include the difficulty of justifying strategic decisions that may appear unorthodox to a leader who does not share your level of insight and is uneasy with you, challenging their adherence to values.

This tension, however, is not without merit. It provides a unique opportunity for accelerated growth, both personally and collectively. Expansive Transformers excel at introspection and real-time adjustment of their actions. By persistently questioning their own assumptions, beliefs, mindsets, behaviors, and emotions, they create a pathway for transitioning to the Integral Transformer Potential, signifying a major evolution in their leadership journey.

Integral Transformer

The Integral Transformer Potential is often regarded as the pinnacle of leadership capability. Leaders who achieve this level possess a remarkable ability to drive outcomes that are profoundly impactful.

The core transition from an Expansive to an Integral Transformer involves a significant enhancement in systemic thinking. While Vision-Centric leaders concentrate on achieving specific outcomes, and Expansive Transformers emphasize interpersonal dynamics, Integral Transformers excel at integrating both aspects seamlessly.

Integral Transformers are adept at engaging effectively with individuals across all levels of Potential. They grasp the comprehensive implications of their decisions, agreements, and actions on the entire organization. Their skill lies in harmonizing diverse groups towards a unified purpose and aligning their company's broader context with these elevated goals.

One of their standout abilities is managing disagreements and conflicts with finesse. Their deep empathy and understanding, whether in individual conversations or group interactions, enable them to uncover and resolve underlying assumptions that participants bring to discussions.

Integral Transformers excel in navigating resistance to change, often originating from deep-seated subconscious fears. They guide transformations within individuals and organizations with a blend of grace and strategic influence rather than relying on authority.

Evidence shows that Integral Transformers are exceptionally well-suited to lead in increasingly complex environments. Clients of mine who have reached this level have made significant contributions, influencing not only their personal realms but also their teams and entire organizations.

As the complexity and unpredictability of the world continue to escalate, senior leaders facing such challenges should consider advancing to the Integral Transformer Potential. Nevertheless, there exists an even rarer stage— the Unitive Transformer Potential—that few have attained.

Unitive Transformer

The Unitive Transformer Potential is exceptionally rare, representing the apex of leadership capability. Leaders who reach this level possess an extraordinary ability to manage multiple, diverse situations simultaneously without succumbing to overwhelm. They adeptly balance long-term visions with immediate needs and are proficient in reinventing both their organizations and the broader communities they serve.

Unitive Transformers are masters of conveying profound truths that deeply resonate with people, engaging both their emotions and intellects. They have a remarkable talent for distilling complex issues into understandable concepts through metaphors and symbols, making the abstract more tangible and relatable. Their adherence to high ethical standards and their inherent integrity draw followers naturally, and their charisma is both magnetic and deeply meaningful.

At the Unitive Transformer level, leaders have the capacity to spearhead and guide large-scale social movements with aspirations for global influence, especially in a world marked by division. Although I have not personally coached any Unitive Transformers, and only a minuscule fraction of leaders (0.1%) reach this level, the transformative impact of historical figures like Martin Luther King Jr., Nelson Mandela, and Mahatma Gandhi offers a tantalizing glimpse into the possibilities. Imagine the profound change that could be achieved if such leaders were at the helm of today's global organizations.

The Bottom Line

It's important to recognize that 85% of the individuals you encounter operate within the Centric Potential. This widespread occurrence presents a considerable opportunity for both personal and organizational advancement. By committing to enhance your own Potential, you can also drive the transformation of your team and organization, fostering a higher level of awareness and performance.

POTENTIAL		PERCENTAGE
Self	Centric	5%
Group		10%
Domain		35%
Vision		30%
Expansive	Transformer	15%
Integral		5%
Unitive		0%

Figure 2.5 – Leaders Potential Distribution

Understanding these levels of Potential not only enhances your leadership capabilities but also empowers you to cultivate a culture of continuous improvement within your sphere of influence. As you progress through the various stages, you become a catalyst for significant change, encouraging a more profound and effective engagement with both challenges and opportunities.

In the upcoming chapter, we will explore actionable strategies for evaluating your own and others' current Potential levels. This will provide you with essential tools to identify starting points for your transformational journey, setting the foundation for ongoing personal and professional growth.

CHAPTER 3.

IDENTIFY YOUR POTENTIAL

Potential Drives Performance

During my extensive experience leading growth in various global companies, I was convinced that a well-crafted strategy paired with impeccable execution was the key to business success. When everything aligned perfectly, I would congratulate myself on my strategic brilliance. However, when things went awry, it was all too convenient to blame market fluctuations or other external factors. This created a repetitive cycle of occasional success and frequent failure, yet I never took the time to critically examine what might truly be missing from the equation.

The full realization came only after I transitioned from the fast-paced corporate world to focus on coaching leadership teams and exploring different performance frameworks. It was during this period that I uncovered a crucial yet often overlooked element: leadership effectiveness. A pivotal moment came when I encountered a study discussed in *Mastering Leadership* by William A. Adams and Robert J. Anderson. This study, analyzing data from 2,000 senior executives, revealed a striking link between leadership effectiveness and business performance. Leaders at the top 10% of companies scored at the 80th percentile in leadership effectiveness, while those at the bottom 10% barely reached the 30th percentile.

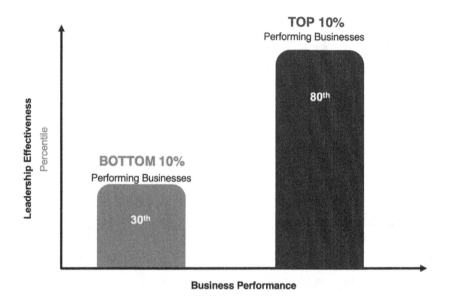

Figure 3.1 - Leadership Effectiveness and Business Performance
(Source: Mastering Leadership, by William A. Adams and Robert J. Anderson)

This realization was a turning point—leadership effectiveness was the critical factor I had previously overlooked. Although I had always understood that leadership was important, I had underestimated its significance, mistakenly believing that if I focused on guiding strategy and execution, everything else would fall into place. Clearly, I was mistaken.

What I discovered was that while vision, strategy, and execution are fundamental, they represent only part of the equation. Crucial components such as systemic awareness, authenticity, self-awareness, and, most importantly, the quality of relationships are essential. Without these elements, true leadership effectiveness remains elusive, and this deficiency inevitably impacts our financial performance.

The Leadership Circle Profile, which we implemented at my firm to assess leadership effectiveness, provided further insights. The profile indicated that 80% of leaders were functioning at what they categorized as 'Reactive' levels—Group and Domain-Centric—while only 15% operated at 'Creative' levels—Vision-Centric and Expansive Transformer—and a mere 5% reached the 'Integral' level, the Integral Transformer.

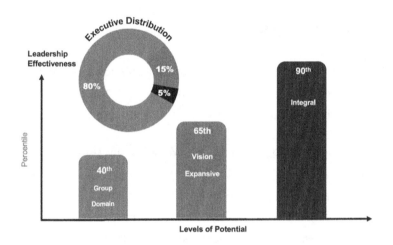

Figure 3.2 – Leadership Effectiveness and Levels of Potentials
(Modified from Mastering Leadership by William A. Adams and Robert J. Anderson)

My Leadership Circle Profile 360 evaluation, conducted by my former colleagues, provided the final insights I needed to complete the puzzle of my career. It became evident that my Potential had not sufficiently developed to meet the demands of leading a multinational organization amidst a landscape of complexity and uncertainty. This realization affirmed a more profound truth: the higher our Potential, the more effective our leadership becomes, and as a result, our business performance improves.

As leaders advance to more Expansive and Integral levels, they not only enhance their ability to make more thoughtful and emotionally intelligent decisions but also foster a deeper connection between their minds and hearts. This evolution enables leaders to embrace the diversity of people and appreciate the intricacies of life in all its complexity.

As we progress through this book, we will delve into methods for assessing and expanding your own Potential, ensuring that you are not merely managing but thriving in your leadership role.

Measuring Potential

Scientists have developed three main approaches for assessing Potential levels. The appendix details how this book's Potential framework aligns with these various methodologies.

The most objective approach is the Washington University Sentence Completion Test (WUSCT), created by Jane Loevinger. This test operates on the premise that our language reflects our level of Potential. It suggests that individuals at different Potential levels will interpret and describe the same events in varied ways based on their distinct perspectives.

Another method is the subject/object interview, pioneered by Harvard professor Lisa Lahey, drawing from Robert Kegan's adult development theory. This technique involves asking targeted questions to explore an individual's worldview. The responses are recorded and transcribed for analysis. A developmental coach reviews how the person interprets situations to gain insights into their meaning-making process. Though less objective than the WUSCT, this method often provides deeply revealing insights. Many clients express surprise when they read their transcripts, frequently remarking, "Wow, I can actually see my thought process!"

The simplest approach is self-assessment. This involves comparing descriptions of the seven Potential levels with your own experiences, especially in high-pressure situations or critical conversations. However, this method tends to be the least accurate. Individuals often select attributes they aspire to or believe they possess rather than those that genuinely represent their everyday behaviors and thought processes.

Framing Your Level of Potential

Understanding your level of Potential requires evaluating how you usually react in different situations, particularly under stress or in relaxed moments. The results from Potential assessments usually categorize your Potential into three specific levels:

1. **Center of Gravity Potential:** This is the level at which you operate most frequently. It represents your default state in a variety of situations.

2. **Fallback Potential:** This refers to an earlier level of Potential that you might revert to, either intentionally or unintentionally, under certain conditions. It's also known as your 'trailing edge.'

3. **Growth Edge Potential:** This is the next level of Potential you are beginning to operate from, but you have not yet fully stabilized. It shows the areas where you are starting to make progress but are not consistently operating at this level.

Identifying your Center of Gravity is essential as it pinpoints where your predominant behaviors, thoughts, and feelings tend to stabilize. By understanding this, you can better focus on your Growth Edge, which will steer your development efforts. This approach aids in broadening your capabilities and gradually elevating your default Potential to a higher level over time.

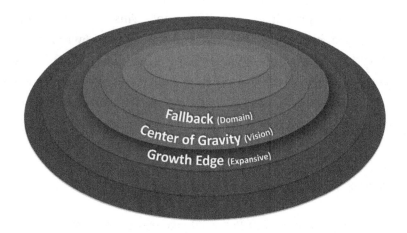

Figure 3.3 – Center of Gravity, Growth Edge, and Fallback

It's Your Turn

Now, let's begin the journey of identifying your Potential. The self-assessment process is straightforward. On a sheet of paper or a digital device, list the seven levels of Potential. As you read through the descriptions of each, mark the level at which you most often operate for each of the following scenarios. At the end of this self-assessment, you'll have a datasheet like this one:

Self

Group   ⁙ ⁙

Domain   ⁙ ⁙ ⁙ ⁙

Vision   ⁙

Expansive

Integral

Unitive

Figure 3.4 – Rate Your Potential

Remember to be honest with yourself. This is not a competition. No one else will see your results, so it's important to reflect genuinely on your behaviors and tendencies.

I recall a humbling experience from a few years back when I took an assessment based on the Washington University Sentence Completion Test (WUSCT). Despite my role as a coach for senior leadership teams and my familiarity with developmental frameworks, I was convinced my Potential had reached the Integral Transformer level. To my surprise, the results indicated that my center of gravity was actually Vision-Centric, with some signs of growth in the Expansive Transformer and noticeable setbacks into Domain-Centric.

This was a significant reality check. I had overestimated my development.

I mostly coached my clients from the Expansive Transformer perspective. Still, when meeting CEOs to offer my services, I operated from the Vision-Centric perspective, focusing on the outcomes I wanted to achieve - closing the deal - and was eager to prove 'how good I was' - the Domain-Centric.

My success rate in closing deals was about 20% when operating primarily from Domain and Vision-Centric Potential. However, it surged to 80% once I evolved into an Expansive and Integral Transformer Potential. Avoid falling into a similar trap. Be conservative in your self-assessment to prevent overestimating your development level.

This self-assessment will help you gain a deeper understanding of how each Potential operates across different contexts. By evaluating your responses to the forthcoming questions, you'll engage in introspection that highlights your dominant Potential levels and areas for growth. Reflect honestly to understand your current position and to chart a course for evolving towards higher levels of Potential.

How Do I Respond to Feedback?

Self-Centric - I fight back, blame others, and retaliate later.

Group-Centric - I deny wrongdoing to avoid disapproval and maintain my image.

Domain-Centric - I defend my expertise and dismiss feedback from those less knowledgeable. I take feedback personally and defend my position.

Vision-Centric - I welcome feedback that helps me achieve my goals and commit to behavioral changes.

Expansive Transformer - I view feedback as essential for uncovering blind spots.

Integral Transformer - I invite feedback to grow, evaluate my contribution to the issue, and see conflict as part of relationships.

Unitive Transformer - I view feedback and compliments as integral to relationships.

How Do I Perceive Control?

Self-Centric - I protect myself from others who want to overpower me.

Group-Centric - I adhere strictly to rules and procedures and ask for approval.

Domain-Centric - I use my expertise, data, and best practices to maintain control.

Vision-Centric - I view myself as the captain, steering all outcomes.

Expansive Transformer - I question the concept of control, seeking broader viewpoints to let go of control.

Integral Transformer - I see control as the choices I make in the context of the broader system.

Unitive Transformer - I own my responsibilities to see multiple stakeholders' underlying needs and choices now, in the past, and in the future.

How Do I Respond When Others Make Mistakes?

Self-Centric - I quickly demote or dismiss those responsible.

Group-Centric - I explain the consequences so they know what they should and shouldn't do.

Domain-Centric - I guide to correct and improve performance.

Vision-Centric - I offer direct feedback, coaching, and growth opportunities.

Expansive Transformer - I seek to understand the underlying reasons and perspectives through their reflections.

Integral Transformer - I explore how our systems, processes, and people contributed to the mistakes.

Unitive Transformer - I consider the broader assumptions and biases that influence perceptions of the mistake.

How Do I View Our Differences?

Self-Centric - I expect others to accept me as is.

Group-Centric - I expect conformity to group norms and values.

Domain-Centric - I see differing views as incorrect, advocating for my own.

Vision-Centric - I accept diverse viewpoints but prioritize alignment with goals.

Expansive Transformer - I see how I became who I am and am curious about others' unique experiences.

Integral Transformer - I reflect on my interactions as feedback for personal growth so that I won't project my lens on others.

Unitive Transformer - I see all perspectives as deeply interconnected as we are ourselves and each other.

How Do I Lead?

Self-Centric - I focus solely on my agenda.

Group-Centric - I enforce rules and expectations.

Domain-Centric - I lead through expertise and efficiency.

Vision-Centric - I guide towards clear goals and outcomes.

Expansive Transformer - I adapt leadership to the needs of the situation.

Integral Transformer - I consider the dynamic needs of the system.

Unitive Transformer - I integrate multiple dimensions in real-time with a spontaneous being.

How Do I Understand Time?

Self-Centric - I focus on immediate threats and opportunities.

Group-Centric - I concentrate on short-term objectives.

Domain-Centric - I manage time as a finite resource that should not be wasted.

Vision-Centric - I optimize my time to maximize efficiency.

Expansive Transformer - I perceive time as elastic, influenced by perception and experience.

Integral Transformer - I consider the impact across various timescales, contexts, and effects.

Unitive Transformer - I view time as an integral, non-dimensional flowing aspect of global, natural, and historical contexts.

How Do I React to Situations?

Self-Centric - I prioritize my immediate desires and needs.

Group-Centric - I adhere to expected norms and behaviors.

Domain-Centric - I apply best practices and expertise.

Vision-Centric - I focus on achieving specific outcomes.

Expansive Transformer - I explore various perspectives to deepen understanding.

Integral Transformer - I seek underlying drivers and systemic, cultural, and relational factors.

Unitive Transformer - I contemplate how my perceptions shape my reality.

What Am I Responsible for?

Self-Centric - I'm responsible for my own needs and desires.

Group-Centric - I'm responsible for doing my job, fulfilling expectations, following the rules, having good relationships, sticking to reporting lines, and maintaining harmony.

Domain-Centric - I'm responsible for doing things right, gathering all the data, acquiring knowledge, and becoming the best.

Vision-Centric - I'm responsible for setting goals, planning strategies, creating processes, measuring results, and analyzing outcomes.

Expansive Transformer - I'm responsible for challenging the status quo and fostering inclusive dialogue with diverse stakeholders.

Integral Transformer - I'm responsible for identifying blind spots, thinking further ahead and back, knowing myself deeply, and creating sustainable practices for all.

Unitive Transformer - I'm responsible for reimagining past and present flow into the future and questioning my and others' stories.

How Do You Respond to People Who Step Out of Line?

Self-Centric - I punish the troublemakers who did it intentionally.

Group-Centric - I reprimand them and suggest corrective action.

Domain-Centric - I educate them about the right way to behave.

Vision-Centric - I seek to understand their reasons and guide them back on track.

Expansive Transformer - I listen and learn from their experiences and motivations.

Integral Transformer - I appreciate their creativity and explore the options for systemic change.

Unitive Transformer - I'm curious about what defined their line. Maybe we should challenge these lines.

How Do I View Relationships?

Self-Centric - I use relationships for personal gain and discard them when they are useless.

Group-Centric - I value relationships for mutual support and avoid conflict to maintain harmony.

Domain-Centric - I prefer relationships with those who can enhance my professional network.

Vision-Centric - I seek beneficial relationships that align with my purpose and vision and provide learning opportunities.

Expansive Transformer - I value deep, judgment-free, and intimate explorations of self and others.

Integral Transformer - I see relationships as opportunities to drive the evolution of myself, ourselves, and society.

Unitive Transformer - I recognize our interconnectedness, shaping and reflecting each other's realities.

How Do You Make Decisions Under Uncertainty?

Self-Centric - I act quickly to control the situation without wasting time on discussions.

Group-Centric - I wait for further information and approvals before we make rush decisions and "rock the boat."

Domain-Centric - I use data, technical specifications, and past experiences to guide decisions.

Vision-Centric - I evaluate all options to ensure impactful decisions.

Expansive Transformer - I consider diverse viewpoints and focus on decision-making experience and discovery processes.

Integral Transformer - I integrate multiple factors, long-term considerations, and unpredictable outcomes.

Unitive Transformer - I delve into underlying assumptions and embrace contradictory actions that will reveal patterns of complexity.

How Do I Influence Others?

Self-Centric - I use any means necessary to ensure victory.

Group-Centric - I encourage conformity and utilize company policies and politics to influence others.

Domain-Centric - I use data, expertise, and detailed proof to argue my position convincingly.

Vision-Centric - I motivate others by setting a clear vision and ambitious goals and explaining the benefits.

Expansive Transformer - I introduce multiple perspectives to enrich discussions and encourage adaptive thinking to shift the paradigm.

Integral Transformer - I influence with powerful purpose, long-term strategy, and the highest integrity.

Unitive Transformer - I influence from behind the scenes as an observer and participant, unfolding paradigm shifts, reframing issues, and holding systemic mirrors.

How Do I Respond to Conflict?

Self-Centric - I respond to conflict head-on to win the situation, retreating only if defeat seems likely.

Group-Centric - I avoid direct conflict within my group, carefully navigating and waiting out tensions.

Domain-Centric - I engage assertively with those who challenge my knowledge, often finding such interactions stressful.

Vision-Centric - I address conflicts constructively, focusing on resolving them in ways that align with our team's objectives.

Expansive Transformer - I explore both sides' perspectives to complement my incomplete views.

Integral Transformer - I embrace conflict as an opportunity for co-creative solutions, generative dialogue, and adaptive views.

Unitive Transformer - I view conflicts as natural dynamics within relationships, influencing and being influenced by them consciously and unconsciously.

How Do I Relate to Others?

Self-Centric - I rely primarily on myself and blame others when things go wrong.

Group-Centric - I support others to secure their appreciation within the group but am selective about whom I help.

Domain-Centric - I prefer interactions with knowledgeable and efficient individuals who get things done; I find unnecessary meetings and small talk frustrating.

Vision-Centric - I build relationships that support our collective goals, valuing effective communication and shared values.

Expansive Transformer - I foster deep, intimate, and judgment-free connections, valuing diverse viewpoints and mutual assumptions questioning.

Integral Transformer - I engage openly and vulnerably, viewing relationships as platforms for shared growth and diverse insights.

Unitive Transformer - I approach relationships with deep compassion, recognizing our interconnected experiences and shared humanity.

What's Most Important for Me?

Self-Centric - Getting what I want, leveraging opportunities, keeping my benefits, and avoiding trouble.

Group-Centric - Keeping stability, harmony, and stress-free acceptance within my community.

Domain-Centric - Leveraging my strengths, promoting my ideas, and being recognized for my expertise.

Vision-Centric - Achieving strategic goals, delivering results, and driving effective outcomes.

Expansive Transformer - Challenging my and our systemic assumptions and exploring new possibilities.

Integral Transformer - Integrating diverse demands to forge deep, principled commitments.

Unitive Transformer - Contemplating the broader implications of our actions on the collective consciousness.

How Do I Relate to Power and Authority?

Self-Centric - I dominate to ensure control and avoid being dominated.

Group-Centric - I respect hierarchical power and expect others to adhere to it.

Domain-Centric - I believe that authority comes from superior knowledge and expertise.

Vision-Centric - I delegate formal and informal power strategically to fulfill organizational roles and goals but hold the ultimate control.

Expansive Transformer - I seek mutual power through persuasion and challenge organizational power norms.

Integral Transformer - I recognize the limitations of power and blend different forms to foster creative resolutions.

Unitive Transformer - I understand the cost of using power unilaterally and strive for equitable interactions.

What Am I Worried About?

Self-Centric - Personal survival, avoiding trouble, and evading consequences.

Group-Centric - Losing social standing, being disliked, or being excluded from the group.

Domain-Centric - Losing respect, appearing incompetent, or being caught without answers.

Vision-Centric - Failing to meet goals or standards and running out of time.

Expansive Transformer - Feeling uncertain about my direction and role within the organization.

Integral Transformer - Missing underlying issues and not fully understanding complex situations.

Unitive Transformer - The long-term impacts of our actions on society and future generations.

What Motivates Me?

Self-Centric - Survive

Group-Centric - Belong

Domain-Centric - Be competent

Vision-Centric - Be effective

Expansive Transformer - Inquire

Integral Transformer - Be the most I can be

Unitive Transformer – Be

How Do I Think?

Self-Centric - The world is a competitive battleground where I must dominate to survive.

Group-Centric - I feel unappreciated and powerless, constrained by group norms.

Domain-Centric - Others often lack understanding and only I know the right way.

Vision-Centric - I make tough decisions and influence others to realize a shared vision.

Expansive Transformer - I recognize multiple realities and question my assumptions.

Integral Transformer - I acknowledge my biases and strive to see beyond them.

Unitive Transformer - I contemplate life's complexities and seek deeper meanings.

How Do I Feel?

Self-Centric - Frequently angry and confrontational.

Group-Centric - Generally content unless my harmony with the group is disrupted.

Domain-Centric - Stressed, often struggling to maintain control.

Vision-Centric - Frustrated when outcomes don't align with my plans.

Expansive Transformer - Curious and empathetic, but sometimes confused.

Integral Transformer - Guided by my emotions to uncover personal insights.

Unitive Transformer - I feel free and at peace.

Sum It Up

You've now marked your responses across twenty different scenarios, distributing "strikes" among various levels of Potential.

Center of Gravity

The level with the highest number of strikes represents your Center of Gravity—the default Potential that influences your everyday decisions and actions in both work and personal contexts. Take a moment to reflect: Does this level align more with your ideals or your reality? If you're unsure, review the Potential descriptors below again and pinpoint the Center of Gravity that genuinely reflects your actual behavior rather than your aspirational self.

Growth Edge

Next, identify your Growth Edge, which is the Potential that follows your Center of Gravity. This is the level with fewer strikes, suggesting that you have the ability to operate from this level under specific circumstances.

As you advance toward your Growth Edge, you'll develop the capacity to consistently and deliberately function at this higher Potential. This progress will enable you to overcome challenges and resolve issues that previously impeded or even stalled your development.

Fallback

Your Fallback, or trailing edge, represents the previous levels of Potential you have surpassed on your way to your Growth Edge. While you have mostly moved beyond this Fallback level, you might occasionally revert to it, particularly under stress or when provoked. This regression can occur unintentionally, such as reverting to a Self-Centric mode in a crisis, or intentionally, like slipping into Group-Centric behavior at a social event when seeking approval.

The survival instincts of the Self-Centric mode are crucial to ensure safety in life-threatening situations. Once that immediate threat is gone, transitioning to Group-Centric allows you to focus on collective well-being. As flight safety announcements go, you need to secure your own oxygen mask before assisting others.

However, these fallbacks can also create challenges, pulling you back into less effective behaviors precisely when you need to be at your best. In the upcoming chapters, we will explore how to recognize when you are slipping into these fallback modes, understand the triggers for such regressions, and develop strategies to manage and transcend these instincts in high-pressure situations. Stay tuned as we uncover ways to maintain control and perform effectively even when faced with adversity.

Validate Your Self-Assessment

To enhance the accuracy of your self-assessment, it's valuable to seek external validation. Take a photo or save the descriptions of the seven levels of Potential, then share them with trusted individuals—such as your partner, colleagues, boss, or close friends. Ask them which level of Potential they most commonly observe in you. This process can offer revealing insights: do their perceptions match your self-assessment?

Having these discussions can lead to meaningful conversations, promote greater transparency, and strengthen your relationships. Additionally, it provides a more comprehensive understanding of how others perceive you and can guide your efforts toward personal growth.

Summary of the Potentials
Self-Centric

- Manipulative, blames others, opportunistically disobeys authority
- Rejects feedback, adheres strictly to own rules, driven by selfish motives
- Operates on a 'win at all costs' mentality with a short-term focus

Group-Centric

- Avoids conflict, pleases others, adheres to norms, and obeys rules without question
- Needs to fit into cultural norms, highly values group acceptance and status
- Prioritizes belonging and being liked over personal desires

Domain-Centric

- Views self as the ultimate expert, problem solver, and source of best practices
- Critical of others and resent feedback except from recognized experts
- Values recognition and indispensability strive to stand out through knowledge

Vision-Centric

- Collaborative, results-oriented, and values long-term effectiveness
- Self-awareness of limiting behaviors aims to align actions with integrity
- Open to feedback, driven by a strong vision, and fosters robust team dynamics

Expansive Transformer

- Maintains high awareness of context and personal assumptions
- Seeks feedback actively and thinks creatively beyond normative standards
- Values interdependence and drives change by connecting disparate ideas and timelines

Integral Transformer

- Systemic thinker, manages paradoxes effectively, and is self-aware of personal flaws
- Comfortable with uncertainty and complexity, reflective and adaptive in real-time
- Balances process and outcomes, fosters high consciousness in self and others

Unitive Transformer

- Embraces metaphorical thinking and recognizes the interconnectedness of all things
- Observes actions from within and without, fostering social shifts and creating movements
- Integrates diverse perspectives, seeing the oneness in diversity and complexity

The Bottom Line

Think of the seven levels of Potential as conceptual markers on our evolutionary journey. Although these levels represent distinct points, the continuum they form has countless Potential stages. By condensing this infinite range into seven clear levels, we can better articulate and visualize our growth trajectory.

Your current frontier, known as the Growth Edge, is where the transformative work occurs. It represents the next stage for your behaviors, mindsets, beliefs, and emotions. Moving into this Growth Edge can greatly improve your leadership effectiveness and overall performance. More importantly, it can foster deeper, more trusted, and meaningful relationships.

Ready to amplify your impact both personally and within your team or organization? Excellent—because in the next chapter, we will explore practical strategies for advancing from your current Potential level to the next. This will help you unlock new capabilities and achieve greater success. Let's begin!

CHAPTER 4.

BOOST YOUR POTENTIAL

The Way to Change

Did you know 70-90% of personal, team, and organizational transformations are unsuccessful? And let's not even start on New Year's resolutions—about 80% of them are forgotten by February each year. Take a moment to consider: How many major changes have you successfully made to your own behavior patterns? And what about those around you?

Change isn't just complicated; it can feel nearly impossible. Why? Because changing behaviors involves more than just deciding to act differently. Our behaviors are deeply embedded in layers of our psyche, anchored by unproven fears and firmly held assumptions. These fears and assumptions set off a chain reaction: they trigger protective mechanisms and constrain our core beliefs, ultimately working against us. These safeguards are meant to protect us but also hold us back from making the transformative changes we seek to achieve.

Why Behavior?

The real test of developing your Potential lies in changing behaviors that others can see. It's easy to delude ourselves into believing we've changed when, in reality, nothing has actually shifted.

I swear I noticed a change in my body when I tried losing weight. The weight scale told me otherwise. I envisioned looking better because I desired it, but the reality was quite different. The external validation of our change is the best method for measuring our progress.

An iceberg metaphor provides an easy way to describe how to maximize our Potential. What you see above the waterline—the 10%—represents our behaviors. Everything below? Our hidden depths – the 90% - are thoughts and feelings that others can't know unless we express them.

To truly elevate our Potential, we need to sync changes across three levels:

Feeling (emotional)

External stimuli evoke emotional responses that vary depending on an individual's level of Potential. The more evolved our Potential, the greater our ability to be aware of and regulate our emotional responses and those of others. At earlier stages of Potential, individuals often respond with automatic emotional reactions. In contrast, at later stages, they develop a space between a stimulus and their response, allowing them time to regulate their emotions and engage in more effective, practical thinking.

Thinking (cognitive)

Stress can trigger instant, often irrational reactions (thank you, amygdala!). Those further along in their Potential development give themselves a pause, allowing time to calm their emotions and reframe their thoughts. This thoughtful pause is crucial for responding more effectively.

Doing (behavioral)

The actions we take in response to stressful stimuli are seen as behaviors. Centric Potentials respond quickly to their emotions, while Transformer Potentials behave in complete detachment from them.

While behaviors are the visible part of the iceberg, how we feel and think—the inner game—steers these outward actions. The inner game runs the outer game. To change what others see, we must transform what they can't - the inner game.

Why Fears?

Fears are intense emotions deeply ingrained in our survival mechanisms as humans. They trigger automatic responses that have kept us safe throughout our evolution. For clarity, let's simplify the brain's complex structure into two main areas: the lower brain (brainstem and diencephalon) and the upper brain (limbic system and cortex).

Here are two intriguing facts:

1. The lower brain processes all sensory information—such as what we see and hear—before it reaches the upper brain. It is like a gatekeeper.
2. The lower brain doesn't differentiate between past, present, and future. It stores past experiences like photos without dates on our smartphones. Only the upper brain can reflect on the past and plan for the future.

Therefore, the lower brain tends to respond to current events in the same way it would have reacted to past experiences, particularly stressful situations or threats that remind it of previous traumas or adversities.

In real-life and death situations, this mechanism can save us. But in day-to-day situations, it fails us. Therefore, knowing our fears is key to changing behaviors.

5 Transformation Elements - The Iceberg Model

To grow our Potential, we need to work on five transformation elements - Identify the **fears** that drive unwanted **behaviors**, the automatic **assumptions** we make, the **safeguards** we count on, and the **beliefs** that narrow our choices.

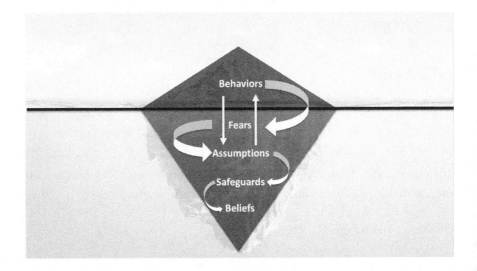

Figure 4.1 – The Iceberg Model

Behaviors, fears, assumptions, safeguards, and beliefs are like forces within the iceberg. Buoyancy, thermal forces, wind, waves, currents, tidal, pressure, and glacial forces cause the iceberg to change shape and size over time and eventually melt and disintegrate. The same is true of the five forces of transformation. They ultimately melt and integrate when you are ready to move to the next level.

Upgrading Your Operating System

Transforming our Potential is like upgrading our operating system. The behaviors we exhibit above the water are like apps that run on the operating system hidden below the waterline. While the apps are visible, the operating system remains out of sight.

If you stop updating your mobile device's operating system, the apps will eventually stop working. Similarly, as work and personal life complexity increases, we stop being effective leaders, parents, and partners unless we upgrade our operating system to the next version of Potential.

Many transformations fail because we try to implement new approaches while still operating with outdated systems. We lack either the patience or the know-how required for upgrading our operating system. Our life's dramas and childhood traumas have molded our operating systems, and our past successes have ingrained specific 'right ways' of doing things in our systems. However, once thriving, these patterns may now be obsolete—what got us here won't get us there.

So, how does personal transformation occur? Developmental psychologists Robert Kegan and Lisa Lahey define transformation as a process of moving from being 'subject' to our experiences to becoming 'object' to them. This shift involves becoming aware of previously unnoticed aspects of ourselves. We transform through:

- Encounters with unfamiliar contexts that challenge our assumptions
- Complex situations that reveal the limits of our knowledge
- Events that contradict our reality
- Experiences opposing our beliefs or values
- Seeing ourselves from a different perspective

Each of these triggers can challenge our understanding of how the world functions. When we perceive the world differently through a new worldview, we reach a new 'station' in our growth journey. This 'station' is not a final destination but an outcome of our transformative work, allowing us to evolve our perspectives.

Decide on a One Big Shift

As we begin our transformation journey, it all starts with identifying one major adaptive change—what we'll call the One Big Shift. It is like the 'mother of all changes.' This shift has the power to unlock a series of other changes, significantly improving how we navigate different aspects of our lives.

In the upcoming chapters, we will explore the specific shifts required to move from one Potential level to the next, our Growth Edge.

Let's begin with some guidelines for selecting your One Big Shift.

Make it adaptive

A true change isn't something you can simply check off your to-do list in a few days; it's adaptive, not technical. Ronald Heifetz, a Harvard University professor, highlights that "The single biggest failure of leadership is to treat adaptive challenges like technical problems."

Here's how he distinguishes between the two:

Technical Problems:

- Easy to identify and solve, often quickly and by experts.
- Solutions are typically straightforward, can be implemented broadly through decisions or directives, and are generally well-received by people.

Adaptive Challenges:

- Hard to recognize and often denied.
- Involve deep changes in values, beliefs, roles, relationships, and approaches.
- Solutions require those affected to engage deeply and are complex, crossing organizational boundaries and demanding shifts in numerous areas.
- People often resist even acknowledging the existence of adaptive challenges, let alone addressing them.

For instance, setting aside an hour each day for strategic thinking might appear meaningful, but it remains a technical change. It doesn't require altering your fundamental behavior. A true adaptive change, like delegating non-strategic tasks, requires deeper behavioral shifts beyond just adjusting your schedule.

Make it about you

Your One Big Shift should focus solely on you—not on others. It must be something that you can fully control and that holds true only for you. For example, saying, "I want people to buy into my ideas," isn't an effective commitment because you can't control whether others accept your ideas. This is why aiming for 'influence' isn't ideal, even though it's an action word. Influence is an outcome, not a behavior change. A more effective behavioral goal might be: "Openly share my purpose and values and express my perspective when there's a misalignment."

Make it affirmative

When my clients review their assessment results, their initial reaction often focuses on what needs to be fixed or stopped, implying that something is broken. However, true development rests on the principle that nothing is inherently broken. Instead, we reframe negatives into positives. For example, instead of saying, "Don't rush to decisions," we shift to "Thoroughly explore and consider all perspectives before making decisions." Likewise, "Don't control the conversation" becomes "Create space for others to share their thoughts." This approach moves the focus from avoidance to proactive engagement.

Make it about the process rather than the outcome

We often drive performance by setting goals as measurable outcomes. However, the outcomes themselves aren't the change. It's crucial to focus on the underlying processes that need to evolve to achieve these outcomes. Instead of aiming to "Become more productive" or "Become more efficient," which are outcome-oriented, we should identify what changes in our behaviors will lead to increased productivity and efficiency. This approach shifts the focus from *what* to achieve to *how* to achieve it. It emphasizes growth and development in our actions and behaviors.

Make it observable

While commitments centered on 'being'—like 'being bold' or 'being confident'—are important, they focus more on the inner self than on behaviors others can see. To make your transformation visible, translate these 'being' goals into observable behaviors. For example, if the goal is to be more curious, instead of just aiming to "be curious," define it as "asking questions instead of making statements." This approach makes your progress more tangible and provides clear criteria for measuring change.

Make it life-changing

When clients set a goal, I encourage them to assess its impact on a scale from 1 to 5—where 1 is trivial and 5 is transformative. Those who scored their goal as transformative said it had a significant impact not only on their professional life but on their personal life. For example, if your goal is to forge deeper connections at work, also consider your relationships at home. We are the same people in both places unless we are putting on a mask in one. A goal that improves both areas of life without masking any part of ourselves can be especially motivating when supported by a strong 'why.' This 'why' should explain the profound impact the change will have on your life and the lives of others.

Make it a growth edge change

To truly expand our capabilities, we need to focus on adopting behaviors that align with our Growth Edge. This is the level of Potential just beyond your current Center of Gravity. These are not just small improvements but significant shifts that can propel you forward in your personal and professional growth. In the second part of this book, we will explore how these shifts can transform the seven levels of Potential. You will learn to identify the key behaviors that mark the next stage in your development journey and how to integrate these into your daily life effectively. This ensures that each step you take is not just progress but a leap toward realizing your full Potential.

Identify Behaviors that Get in the Way

After choosing your One Big Shift, the next essential step is to identify behaviors that block this change. These are the action verbs from your current level of Potential (Center of Gravity) that prevent growth toward your next level (Growth Edge). The counterproductive behaviors are observable actions, not vague concepts or emotions.

Consider this scenario: imagine reviewing footage of yourself from the past week. Reflect on moments that led to frustration or disappointment, what I call "oh shit!" moments. What specific actions—or lack thereof—contributed to these reactions? Identifying these behaviors is crucial because they directly affect your ability to achieve your One Big Shift.

Connecting with Your Fears

Uncovering our fears is crucial for developing our Potential. These fears are hidden beneath the surface, much like the submerged part of an iceberg. To truly understand and address them, you must go beyond superficial engagement and dive deep—like scuba diving into your psyche.

My 20-year military service made me prone to suppressing my fears, to the point where I started to believe my own facade. My colleagues even called me "Dave the Brave," which didn't help. I wasn't brave; I just couldn't connect with my fears buried under layers of self-deception. It wasn't until I began to identify my fears that I started to evolve as a leader, husband, father, friend, and coach.

How to identify your fears?

After identifying behaviors that obstruct your desired shift, reflect on what worries or stresses you about doing the opposite. Dive deep to uncover the subconscious fears that are holding you back:

- What is the worst thing that could happen?
- What risks are involved?

For instance, I coached a charismatic CEO who led his senior leadership team with a firm hand. His Growth Edge involved learning to delegate and share power. Here are some counter behaviors and the fears associated with changing them:

- **Counter behavior:** Giving my opinion too quickly
- **Fear:** Losing my status as the primary driver of the business
- **Counter behavior:** Not asking questions
- **Fear:** Revealing that I don't have all the answers
- **Counter behavior:** Taking too much air time in meetings
- **Fear:** Losing ownership
- **Counter behavior:** Cut people off
- **Fear:** Not getting the results I want the way I want them

You can see how subconscious fears held back this successful CEO and blocked his Potential to scale the business further. Until we address the underlying fears driving our counterproductive behaviors, we won't be able to unlock our full Potential.

To truly connect with your deeper fears, visualize yourself not doing or doing the opposite behaviors. What emotions arise? What concerns surface?

It's crucial to fully experience these unsettling emotions before writing them down. If you don't delve deep enough, you won't be able to decode other parts of your operating system—like assumptions, safeguards, and beliefs. Fears are the key.

Ask yourself: "What's at risk for me?" and "What's the worst that could happen?" Identifying these fears requires feeling vulnerable and exposed to possible threats, getting to the root of your primal fears of being defenseless.

Here are more examples of common fears:

- Being out of control
- Being wrong
- Being excluded
- Looking incompetent
- Looking stupid
- Looking weak

Distinguish between fears that relate to how you perceive yourself ('being' fears) and how others perceive you ('looking' fears). For example, my biggest fear was "not being good enough," which led me to exhibit counterproductive bragging behaviors to mask the feelings associated with this fear.

Construct Restraining Assumptions

Assumptions are the unquestionable narratives we subconsciously accept and rarely challenge. Many of these assumptions form during earlier life stages—childhood, adolescence, college, and early career. They are the imprints of past experiences that have shaped us but may no longer serve us well.

These assumptions are deeply ingrained, so much so that we often aren't aware of their influence. We become unwitting hostages to these assumptions, which can hijack our actions without our conscious realization. They are our most significant blind spots, keeping us stuck in our current Potential and preventing us from moving forward.

Developing our Potential **makes the unseen seen**—what Robert Kegan called the move 'from subject to object.' When we start to see the assumptions we were previously subject to, they become objects we can examine, and they no longer control us implicitly. It's a shift from seeing through the invisible assumptions (subject) to seeing the assumptions themselves (object).

Identifying these assumptions doesn't require an overwhelming dive into every thought we have. Instead, focus on the assumptions that keep us anchored to our current Potential and prevent us from evolving. One effective method to uncover these assumptions is to listen for "if...then" statements in our internal dialogues. These often reveal the deep-seated assumptions guiding our behavior:

- The 'if' part describes a behavior we avoid.
- The 'then' part outlines the feared consequence of engaging in that behavior.

For example:

- If I listen open-heartedly to others, then I won't be the smartest person in the room.
- If I call out issues, then others may see me as a downer or not a team player.
- If I challenge the CEO, then I risk being belittled.
- If I speak up, then I will be seen as confrontational.
- If I take a stand in disagreement or conflict, then I won't be liked and lose respect.
- If I step into other people's territories, then I'll damage working relationships.
- If I set boundaries, then I'll be seen as unsupportive.
- If I address the elephants in the room, then I'll get into trouble.
- If I ask too many questions, I will be bypassed, won't get credit, or lose the argument.
- If I display emotions, then I'll be unprofessional.

Every level of Potential harbors its own unique set of assumptions. Leaders at the same level of Potential often share similar assumptions. As you progress through this book, you'll find detailed discussions on assumptions relevant to each level of Potential, offering a roadmap for deeper personal growth.

To start addressing these assumptions, identify a few that resonate most deeply with you. Which assumption challenges you the most? Begin there, and actively observe how this assumption influences your reactions in various situations. Pay close attention to the people, environments, and contexts that trigger these assumptions.

Years ago, I faced a significant challenge with an intimidating chairman, which triggered my deep-seated "not good enough" assumption. Despite my typical confidence, this experience underscored the universal nature of assumption triggers. Understanding your own triggers can be a profound step in expanding your Potential. Make it your mission to identify and confront these triggers, turning your insights into actionable growth.

Immunity to Change

In their book *Immunity to Change*, developmental psychologists Robert Kegan and Lisa Lahey explore the crucial role of assumptions in personal and collective change. They describe a self-defending subconscious mechanism that prevents us from achieving our most desired behavior changes, which they call "Immunity to Change."

Imagine pressing the accelerator with one foot while the other foot subconsciously presses the brake. We're not moving forward, but we're wasting gas, making noise, and wearing out the tires. When we become aware of this and lift the foot from the brake, we start to move forward.

Our biological immune system protects us from harmful invaders like bacteria and toxins. However, when we need an organ transplant, the immune system rejects the foreign organ. The One Big Shift is like a foreign organ to our psychological 'immune system' that rejects it to "protect" us.

Kegan and Lahey emphasize that to overcome this immunity, we must challenge and disprove the Big Assumptions driving our anti-change behaviors. By disconfirming these assumptions, we strip them of their power. This involves conducting small, safe-to-fail experiments to test the Big Assumption, proving to our subconscious that it was wrong.

It's crucial, however, not to test assumptions where the possible consequences are too severe. Assumptions like "If I speak out, I'll be fired" or "If I speak out, my wife will divorce me" are too risky. Instead, focus on less severe precursors to these consequences. For example, testing the assumption that "If I speak out, they will get mad at me" is more manageable. This approach allows us to safely challenge and ultimately change our deep-seated fears without facing unacceptable risks.

Release Confining Safeguards

Our deeply held assumptions generate powerful safeguards. These unconscious safeguards protect us from a distorted view of reality. They are like heavy chains that keep us anchored to our current Potential and prevent us from growing. People don't resist change because they don't want to. They resist because they can't turn off or get rid of the safeguards their subconscious mind creates to 'protect' them.

Ironically, these safeguards often hinder rather than help. The biggest safeguards holding back even my CEO clients are related to identity and self-worth.

Identity and self-worth

We go the extra mile to safeguard three types of identity and self-worth:

Results

When our identity (ego) and self-worth depend on accomplishments, successes, and outcomes, we tend to be highly controlling. When outcomes are great, we feel great. When things go badly, there is an immediate threat to our identity and self-worth. We then deflect the failure by blaming our team, bosses, or the economy—anything but ourselves.

This controlling tendency is common among CEOs who have not expanded their Potential beyond the Vision-Centric level and still have a stronghold in the Domain-Centric level. These controlling CEOs lead autocratically because they want to control the outcomes. While they are highly ambitious, their results-driven identity and self-worth hinder their ability to build effective relationships at work and at home.

Intellect

When our identity and self-worth depend on being smart, we argue endlessly and must always be right. If our self-worth depends on our intellect, we show up as critical, arrogant, and distant. When people accept our ideas, we feel great and smart, but when we're wrong—though this rarely happens—we feel unworthy.

Leaders with this tendency are genuinely smart; it's not just a perception. This tendency often develops from a young age when teachers and parents frequently praise us with statements like, "You're so smart." Over time, this becomes ingrained in our identity. It's a gift and a curse. Arrogant and critical behaviors repel others. People, even our kids, can't thrive around us if they feel they "aren't good enough."

One of my clients, a Stanford Ph.D. and math prodigy since age 16, struggled to keep jobs in Silicon Valley despite his exceptional intelligence. It's difficult to work with someone whose identity demands they always be right. When identity and self-worth depend on both outcomes and intellect, it creates a perfect storm: "I know better what we should do (intellect), so just do it my way (control)."

Relationship

When our identity and self-worth depend on relationships, we avoid conflict because we want to please others and maintain harmony. Such leaders often appear passive. They speak less in meetings, observe where those in power and the group are heading, and align with that direction. Leaders who build their identity and self-worth on relationships might say things like, "I don't want to rock the boat" or "I pick my battles." These leaders are often stuck in the Group-Centric Potential and exhibit similar behaviors at home, avoiding confrontation with spouses, kids, or parents even when they have significant concerns.

The most surprising data I see in clients' 360° assessments is that people often get the opposite outcomes of their deepest needs. Those who focus on pleasing others end up struggling to connect with people. The critical individuals who strive to be the smartest in the room have difficulty influencing others. And those who aim to control outcomes often fail to achieve the results they want.

Controlling leaders may excel in many leadership roles but are poor at building relationships. Pleasing leaders often struggle to achieve business goals and are not typically found in business-generating positions. When an operating system ties identity and self-worth to relationships and intellect, people often appear distant and aloof. Conversely, when identity and self-worth are tied to control and intellect, leaders tend to have poor relationships.

Footholds

Footholds are a rock-climbing metaphor for safeguards that keep us anchored in our current position when reaching for the next foothold seems too risky. The bigger the gaps between footholds, the greater the fear of moving forward. We tend to stay where we are, clinging to the familiar.

Footholds are like mantras subconsciously imprinted in our minds, accepted as truths. Many of these "truths" were learned at a young age and continue to influence us. For example:

"Good things come to those who wait."
"What doesn't kill you makes you stronger."
"Pick the low-hanging fruit first."

"All roads lead to Rome."
"No such thing as bad publicity."
"You can't make an omelet without breaking some eggs."
"No pain, no gain."
What foothold do you hang to? Is it time to let go?

Equals

Equals are different types of safeguards where we fuse two things together and use them interchangeably without realizing it. They function like math equations. For example, a common equal involves our beliefs about what success means to us. Here are a few examples:

"Success = making X million by my 40th birthday"

"Success = becoming a CEO by 40"

Sometimes, equals are hidden as unspoken truths that subtly control our thinking. For instance, one of my clients realized that his equal was "Disagreement = Mistrust." He discovered that he didn't trust people who weren't on the same page with him.

Rules

Similar to equals, rules are ways of thinking that unconsciously guide our actions. People who are subject to rules frequently use terms like 'should,' 'must,' and 'would.' For example:

"I should have discussed it with the CEO before sharing it with my peers."
"You should tell me before you inform others."
"You should not discuss issues with my direct reports without keeping me in the loop."

Rules exist only in Centric Potentials, primarily at the Group and Domain-Centric leaders. More examples of Potential-specific rules are in part 2.

Pair Your Beliefs with Interdependent Beliefs

Centric Potentials often cling to single, isolated values, rejecting opposing values and forcing a choice between them. In contrast, Transformer Potentials recognize pairs of interdependent values, moving from an "either/or" mindset to a more inclusive "both/and" perspective.

The key to transitioning from a Centric to a Transformer Potential is acknowledging these interdependent counter-beliefs. Often, when we or others emphasize what's deemed most important, another significant belief or value may be unintentionally overlooked. These seemingly conflicting beliefs, values, strategies, or competencies are known as paradoxes or polarities.

Recognizing and harnessing these polarities is a critical skill that distinguishes Transformer leaders from Centric leaders. It allows them to see beyond traditional dichotomies and leverage a full spectrum of perspectives and strengths.

Polarities

A polarity consists of two related, interdependent beliefs that appear to be in competition, making us feel we must choose one over the other. However, our Potential evolves when we embrace both equally. Transformative change is achieved by leveraging both poles and adopting a "both/and" rather than an "either/or" mindset.

As we explore transformations into specific Potentials, we will delve deeper into identifying the relevant polarities common at each developmental stage. Here are a few examples of such polarities:

- Direct AND Empathetic
- Cautious AND Bold
- Tactical AND Strategic
- Centralization AND Decentralization

By embracing these polarities, we can foster a more balanced and effective approach to leadership and decision-making.

How to Spot Polarities

Identifying polarities often starts by recognizing "either/or" statements and exploring if they can be transformed into "both/and" opportunities. For example, if faced with the choice, "Are we having Chinese or Indian for dinner?" you might think it's an "either/or" decision when dining out. However, if ordering delivery, you could enjoy dishes from both cuisines, embracing a "both/and" approach.

Another way to spot polarities is by noting transitions described as "from ____ to ____." These often involve shifts in values, competencies, or strategies, where "from" indicates the current state and "to" the desired future state. I coached a leader who aimed to transition from being authoritative to being vulnerable. Being solely authoritative led to intimidation and disengagement, while being only vulnerable caused delays and perceived indecisiveness. By leveraging both authority and vulnerability, they mitigated the drawbacks of each approach and harnessed the strengths of both.

As we evolve from Centric to Transformer Potentials, recognizing and managing polarities becomes crucial. In subsequent chapters, I will highlight typical polarities for each Potential and offer strategies for effectively leveraging them.

Polarities vs. Problems

We often mistake polarities for problems, especially in complex situations. This confusion can lead us to fruitlessly try to solve what are essentially unsolvable or wicked problems. Unlike problems, which typically have clear solutions—where you choose one option over another—polarities lack definitive resolutions and are inherently unsolvable. Problems are usually time-bound and have an endpoint, while polarities are ongoing and enduring.

For example, consider a straightforward business problem like a drop in sales. This problem can be addressed with specific solutions such as implementing a new marketing strategy, improving product quality, or reducing prices. Once the appropriate action is taken, the problem can be considered resolved.

In contrast, a polarity such as work-life balance isn't something that can be permanently resolved; it demands ongoing effort to manage the tensions between these two aspects.

Recognizing the difference between polarities and problems is essential. Treating polarities as if they were problems to be solved can lead to wasted resources, frustration, and ineffective strategies. By understanding polarities for what they are, we can manage them more effectively, leveraging the strengths of each side without getting trapped in a futile search for a final solution.

Integration is Key to Transformation

Integrating our Fallback Potentials into our current Growth Edge Potential is crucial for transformation. Instead of viewing this as moving to a new home, think of it as expanding your existing home. The new space represents your emerging Potential, while the original rooms—your earlier stages—remain valuable and active parts of the structure.

Resisting these earlier stages of Fallback Potential can hinder your transformation. From my experiences and observations, I've seen how frustrating it can be to fall back into old behaviors we thought we had outgrown. Embracing compassion for our former selves helps integrate these earlier Potentials into who we are today. Accepting our earlier Potential is crucial for moving forward to the next Growth Edge.

A sign of successful integration is the ability to look back and laugh at our past shortcomings, indicating readiness to continue our developmental journey.

It's important not to skip the foundational chapters in favor of jumping directly to the Center of Gravity chapter. These early chapters are vital for successfully integrating your earlier Potentials into your Center of Gravity, enhancing your chances of a successful transformation.

Part of this integration process involves reflecting on past events and circumstances that shaped our previous behaviors. What made sense then may not apply now. Be kind and compassionate toward your younger self; you have since evolved. It may be time to invite your earlier self to comfortably reside within the expanded spaces of your current Potential.

Transformation Process

The term 'transformation' has become so clichéd that discussing it often feels uncomfortable. Many self-proclaimed experts promise rapid, transformative changes, but in reality, transformation is a demanding and lengthy journey that requires time, effort, patience, and deep introspection. It's not a single event but a continuous process that can span years, decades, or even a lifetime.

Simply reading a book won't bring about transformation. True change happens by applying learned strategies one Potential at a time. In every transformation, the strengths that once anchored your Center of Gravity paradoxically become limitations at your Growth Edge.

This means letting go of strengths that have previously served you well to embrace the capabilities needed for the next level. As we evolve, our current strengths often turn into weaknesses, making the process of transformation particularly challenging. It's daunting to relinquish what has been effective for years, especially when moving into a new phase of life.

We tend to cling to our past and present strengths even when their effectiveness wanes. Old habits are stubborn; it's difficult to shed behaviors that have dominated our actions for many years, and even tougher to adopt new ones.

To emphasize: The strengths of your Center of Gravity become the weaknesses of your Growth Edge. The transformation process involves swapping your old strengths for new ones suited to your Growth Edge. Fortunately, you're not losing these old strengths but integrating them. They remain accessible and can be used when necessary, but your new Growth Edge will guide your decisions and actions.

As you navigate the integration of earlier Potentials, it's important to appreciate, acknowledge, and value each of these early stages. Remember, your kids, partner, colleagues, friends, or parents might be experiencing their own stages of early Potential. Through your journey, you can discover and appreciate the value in each of these stages.

The Bottom Line

Potential development provides a practical and dynamic roadmap for both leadership and personal growth throughout your life. A wealth of scientific evidence shows that the broader your Potential, the stronger your performance—both individually and collectively.

The key to successful transformation is updating your operating system to ensure that new applications are not running on an outdated operating system. The following chapters will explore specific transformations, detailing the five critical components of this operating system: behaviors, fears, assumptions, safeguards, and beliefs.

A crucial prerequisite for successful transformation is integration. This involves consolidating all previous levels of Potential and forming deep connections to each. Integration helps you recognize when you might be regressing, whether intentionally or unintentionally.

Understanding and integrating earlier Potentials not only facilitates your own transformation but also enhances your ability to support others at different stages of their Potential development, including direct reports, peers, and children.

I look forward to hearing about your transformation journey in the future.

PART 2

CENTRIC POTENTIAL TRANSFORMATIONS

CHAPTER 5.

FROM SELF TO GROUP-CENTRIC

Grace is the VP of People Operations at a Silicon Valley tech company. Her role involves aligning employee performance with company goals, managing performance, and fostering engagement and recognition.

Grace hates bad news, but her recent meeting with her boss, the Chief People Officer, was all bad news. Her boss informed her that Stan, the Director of Analytics, would report to her, effective immediately.

Any other person would have been better news. But Stan is a piece of work. Despite being a brilliant techie who can turn data into valuable insights, Stan is difficult to work with. He is known for manipulating others to focus solely on his preferences. Grace suspected he might be abusive, especially towards women, but she lacked concrete evidence. However, Stan had one quality that made him untouchable: he was the founder's nephew, a classic case of nepotism.

In contrast, Grace is known for her kindness. She works hard to please everyone, both at work and at home. She loves working with her team and has built strong relationships with them.

Her team excels in routine HR tasks, but her boss wanted her to be more strategic and forward-thinking in the disruptive era of AI. "It's not enough to meet business needs. You need to anticipate them," she was told repeatedly. "Stan will help you with that."

Grace knew this wasn't true but kept quiet. She wasn't aware that Stan had become unmanageable in his last two roles, and no one else would tolerate him except for Grace, who always says yes.

When Grace told her team about the new addition, they reacted strongly. "No way. This will ruin us!" they exclaimed.

After calming down, the team devised a plan. They decided their strength was as a unit, while Stan was an individual contributor with issues working with others. They agreed there would be no one-on-one meetings with Stan, even with Grace as his manager. All conversations and decisions would be handled by the group, believing that their collective power was their best strategy for managing him.

Together, they agreed on a three-point plan:

1. They wrote down a set of behaviors and rules of engagement for individuals and the team, allowing the group members to vote out any person.
2. They created a bonus compensation plan based primarily on the behaviors of their team.
3. They decided to have a monthly mini-survey of their behaviors and review it in their meetings.

The first month was tough. Stan tried to 'divide and conquer' but couldn't break the team's determination. He focused mainly on his compensation and his fear that the team might vote him out. He also disliked the data captured by the mini-survey about his behavior.

Despite his efforts, Stan never managed to meet with Grace alone. He was forced to work with the team members to navigate this challenging situation.

A year later, Stan had become a valued member of HR, no longer shifting between departments. Grace leveraged the strengths of her Group-Centric Potential to help Stan, previously Self-Centric, elevate his Potential to the next level.

Self to Group-Centric Recollection

Let's revisit our adolescence and think about how our Self-Centric Potential shaped our behaviors.

Many of us shift towards a Group-Centric Potential in high school, often through team sports or trying to fit into popular groups. However, some of us, like me, resisted this change and stayed Self-Centric throughout high school.

At my high school, basketball was the main team sport. I, however, chose table tennis as my competitive sport. I wasn't the worst player on the basketball team, but I practiced basketball only a small fraction of the time I dedicated to table tennis. It wasn't about my skill level; I wanted to win on my own. That's the essence of individual sports.

Looking back, I regret being so self-centered during adolescence, especially compared to my friends, who had already developed a Group-Centric mindset. It was only when I combined my early Potentials that my regret turned into understanding and appreciation for my Self-Centric self and the role this stage played in shaping who I am today.

Take a moment to reflect on how Self-Centric behaviors appeared in your own adolescence. Write down these experiences as you integrate your Self-Centric past into your current Potential.

Self-Centric Strengths

Only 5% of leaders operate at this Potential, but their impact is significant. These leaders are often found in family-owned businesses, where the company was either founded or inherited by a Self-Centric leader. Unlike most of us, who had to adapt to teams and organizations, these leaders didn't need to evolve to the next level. Self-Centric leaders have also become presidents of countries, and you might think of some well-known figures who fit this description. Here are some of the Self-Centric Potential strengths:

Acting fast: Self-Centric leaders are not afraid to act, and they act quickly. This trait sometimes allows them to win big while others are still in paralysis-analysis mode.

Realizing Opportunities: Self-Centric leaders are opportunists. This strength can be valuable in roles such as individual contributor sales representatives in certain industries.

Taking advantage of power: Self-Centric leaders are sensitive to power dynamics and use their positions effectively. If their job goals align with their personal needs and priorities, they can often achieve them, even with their limitations.

Cutting corners: Self-Centric leaders often do not follow rules, which sometimes leads to unexpected, out-of-the-box successes.

Win-driven: The Self-Centric Potential is highly driven by power, status, and perks. They are attracted to commission-based jobs, and leveraging commissions can influence their behavior.

However, be careful. When they win big, it often turns out that they gave false promises, provided inaccurate information, or offered prices outside of policy.

Falling Back

I have always enjoyed science fiction and dystopian books and movies. When the COVID-19 pandemic hit in 2020, the frightening images of violence, riots, and chaos from these stories triggered my Self-Centric Potential. I reverted to a survival mode, driven by a deep fear of an existential threat. Anyone without a mask seemed like an existential threat. The pandemic revealed how easily life events can cause us to fall back.

Not only did my fears not come true, but the opposite happened. The dystopian stories underestimated our society's ability to be kind, generous, and supportive during tough times.

This taught me a valuable lesson. I had always disliked my Self-Centric Potential and overlooked its survival skills. However, this Potential is a part of me, and it's important to acknowledge it.

Think about a time when you fell back into your Self-Centric Potential. Reflect on that period and recognize the role of this Potential within you.

Group-Centric Strengths

The transformation from Self-Centric to Group-Centric is significant, as the behaviors are distinctly different.

Community glue: Group-Centric individuals bring a strong sense of harmony, loyalty, and belonging to organizations, communities, and families. Those who operate at this Potential often see themselves as the glue that holds everything together, acting as the 'soul' of the organization.

Following norms: They conform to group norms and routines without question, aiming to do things the 'right way' to avoid making mistakes.

When you talk to a Group-Centric individual, you can sense that they have a clear sense of what is right and what is wrong.

Loyal to the group: Their mantra is "We're in this together." They are deeply loyal to the group's purpose and shared values. If the group faces challenges, they redouble their efforts to support the team, family, or community.

Respect tradition: Group-Centric leaders profoundly respect tradition and tend to be conservative to preserve these traditions.

Considerate: They are considerate of the needs of others and always ready with good advice, whether asked for or not.

Trust authority: They trust management to make the right decisions and respect hierarchy, status symbols, and authority.

Group-Centric leaders excel in support roles such as customer service, customer success, and human resources.

Decide on the One Big Shift

Potential represents a set of behaviors, with some being strengths and others being weaknesses. Changing multiple behaviors at once is not practical.

Start by choosing one behavior from the next Potential that interests you. This becomes your One Big Shift. Next, identify the counter behaviors that counteract this shift. These counter behaviors are the weaknesses of your current Potential.

To move from Self-Centric to Group-Centric, choose one key behavior from the Group-Centric strengths and outline the corresponding Self-Centric weaknesses.

Even if you have already outgrown the Self-Centric or Group-Centric Potential, understanding this transformation process is beneficial. It allows you to integrate past experiences with your current Potential. It can help you also assist others, particularly Self-Centric individuals, such as teenage children.

Here are a few possible One Big Shifts from Self-Centric to Group-Centric:

- Following rules and procedures
- Looking after colleagues, friends, and family
- Addressing the needs of others
- Inviting people to collaborate

Identify Counter Behaviors

The counter behaviors that work against the One Big Shift are the weaknesses of the Self-Centric Potential:

- Forcing my way
- Winning at all costs
- Doing whatever works for me
- Not revealing weaknesses
- Protecting my turf. ("It belongs to me")
- Taking credit and bragging
- Exposing other people's weaknesses
- Getting angry quickly and losing it easily
- Blaming others
- Manipulating others

Recognizing these counter behaviors can help you uncover the underlying fears, assumptions, safeguards, and beliefs.

Fears are the first layer beneath the surface. Identifying these fears helps us understand the motivations behind counter behaviors. Fears are the intense, distressing emotions that Self-Centric individuals experience when trying to adopt Group-Centric behaviors. For example, they may fear not being able to impose their will or not doing what works best for themselves.

The main fear for Self-Centric individuals is the fear of survival. They often appear aggressive because they are trying to protect themselves. You can associate their behaviors with survival fears when you hear them say:

- "It's a jungle out there."
- "It's a dangerous world."
- "I can't trust anyone."
- "It's me or them."
- "I don't give a shit."

Here are some fears that drive the counter behaviors:

- Staying out of trouble
- Losing the game
- Surviving
- Not getting caught
- Being eliminated
- Being dominated
- Being blamed

Now that we have connected to the fears that interrupt the shift into Group-Centric, let's unfold the assumptions in which these fears are grounded.

Construct Restraining Assumptions

When you understand the behaviors and fears, it's easier to identify the assumptions underlying them. Assumptions are combinations of behaviors and fears structured as:

If (Behavior), Then (Fear)

Assumptions are the stories our subconscious mind creates to avoid fears and their worst-case scenarios. When you link behavior to fear, you reveal the assumptions behind them.

Here are a few examples to help you develop your own versions:

- If I tell the truth, I'll be eliminated.
- If I follow orders, I'll lose.
- If I take care of others, they'll eliminate me.
- If I collaborate with others, I won't survive.
- If I address other people's needs, they'll dominate me.
- If I'm honest, they will use it against me.
- If I do what they want, they will blame me.
- If I work with them, they will use me.

Think back to similar assumptions that may have influenced your actions at various points in your life. You likely don't have those same assumptions now, right? That's because you moved beyond the Self-Centric stage years ago.

We made this transformation by trying new behaviors on a small scale without taking major risks. To our surprise, not only did nothing bad happen, but things often turned out well.

This process is essential for transformation. By identifying our assumptions, we can test them in a small and safe way and prove them wrong. When we disprove these assumptions, our subconscious mind learns that the fears that have held us back are not valid anymore. However, assumptions aren't the only obstacles; we also create safeguards to protect ourselves from these assumptions.

Release Confining Safeguards

Safeguards are self-protective mechanisms designed to guard against the worst-case scenarios our assumptions predict. They are subconscious commitments we make to shield ourselves from fears, but they can also limit our growth. By uncovering these safeguards, we can understand our internal processes and recognize the false reality and untrue nature of these protections.

Identity

We automatically protect ourselves from threats to our identity, feeling safer when our identity is secure. However, growth requires us to let go of our current identity and adopt a new one, and sometimes even take on multiple identities as we move through different Potentials. Self-Centric individuals identify themselves with their wants, needs, and wishes, believing:

- "I am my wants and needs."
- "I am successful if what I wish happens."
- "I do whatever works for me."

Self-Worth

We also protect our sense of worthiness, feeling safe when we believe we are worthy and unsafe when our self-worth is threatened. Our evolutionary development has equipped us with reactive instincts to respond to any perceived threat. As we advance our Potential, we improve our ability to distinguish real threats and separate them from our identity and self-worth.

Self-Centric individuals feel worthy as long as they get what they want. For example, if they buy a new car, they feel great about themselves. But if they don't get what they want, they often react with hostility and anger. This behavior is immature, and while 95% of us outgrow it during our teenage years, 5% carry it into adulthood.

Footholds

Footholds are notions that keep us anchored to our current Potential and prevent us from growing. They act like tethers that hold us back. Can you recall using some of the following Self-Centric phrases when you were younger? Do you hear these phrases from people around you now?

- "Showing weakness is dangerous."
- "It's me against everybody else."
- "Don't kid yourself; everybody takes care of themselves."
- "Are you with me or against me?"
- "I'm not a sucker."
- "They won't take advantage of me or use me."
- "It isn't my problem."

Equals

A quick reminder: "equals" refers to two different things that we often use interchangeably without realizing it. We may not be aware that, subconsciously, we consider these two things to be the same. Some of the Self-Centric equals are:

- Material things = success
- My territory, team, family = my ownership, belongings, stuff
- Power = money
- Success = luck, chance
- Losses = collateral damage

Rules

Self-Centric individuals create internal rules to guide their actions, often without realizing that these rules limit their ability to consider alternative approaches. Here are some Self-Centric rules that hold back the shift into Group-Centric:

- "Rules are created to be broken."
- "I decide on the rules."
- "I'll find loopholes."
- "I avoid punishment."
- "The less they know, the better."
- "If things work, it's me. If they don't work, it's them."

By identifying and challenging these safeguards, we can release their hold on us and facilitate our transformation to a higher Potential.

Pair Beliefs with Interdependent Beliefs

The stronger our safeguards, the more rigid the one-sided beliefs we hold. Beliefs come in pairs, not as identical twins, but as opposites. Each belief has an interdependent counterpart, which is defined in contrast and often seen as its opposite.

Self-Centric individuals see the world in black-and-white terms, with everything being either/or:

- It's them or me
- I win or lose
- It's for me or against me
- It's my way or no way

As you integrate the Self-Centric within yourself or help others transition from Self-Centric to Group-Centric, look for the interdependent beliefs and consider how to use both effectively.

For example, Self-Centric individuals often act immediately, sometimes impulsively, without much thought. Instead of asking them to stop reacting quickly and start thinking before acting, help them incorporate both responses: act now and act later. They don't need to give up the 'now' for the 'later'; they can add the 'later' to the 'now' and have two ways to respond.

This approach forms the basis for transforming belief systems. We don't abandon our current beliefs; instead, we add new ones and integrate them. We pair a dependent belief with an interdependent belief, creating a balance between them. We don't force a shift from individual success (dependent belief) to group success (interdependent belief). We combine 'we' with 'me' and leverage both. We take care of ourselves, AND we take care of others.

Here are a few examples of paired beliefs we want to integrate. The left value is the existing (dependent) belief, and the right value is the new (interdependent) belief. AND (in capital letters) represents the polarity:

- Urgency AND patience
- Skepticism AND trust
- My wants AND other people's wants
- Protect myself AND protect others
- Survive AND Thrive

Reflect on your younger self. Have you noticed any of these values in your actions? Are they fully integrated into who you are now? Do you still prefer one value over the other? By recognizing and integrating these pairs, we can develop a more balanced and holistic approach to our beliefs and behaviors.

My Self-Centric Transformation

Earlier, I shared how I clung to my Self-Centric Potential throughout high school, avoiding groups and team sports. Then, I began dreaming of becoming a fighter pilot. I imagined that fighter pilots flew jets alone, which seemed perfect for my Self-Centric world.

In 1978, I joined the Israeli Air Force Flight Academy. On the first day of basic training, we were met with bad news. The officers told us they would observe each of us closely and cut 85% of the program participants. The most important criterion for staying was how well we supported others during tough times.

I was determined to succeed, but I needed to quickly transform into a Group-Centric Potential. Although I didn't realize it at the time, looking back, I see how my Self-Centric motivation pushed me to make this change rapidly.

It was similar to a skilled Aikidoka neutralizing a larger opponent by blending with their energy rather than opposing it. My Self-Centric drive to win for myself helped me become part of a group. To meet the new requirements, I had to confront my fears, challenge my assumptions, let go of my safeguards, and add new values to my existing ones. There are no shortcuts in transformation.

How did I manage to transform in just a few days? Like in the story of Stan and Grace, the group was the catalyst. This was a unique group I had never encountered before. Half of the flight academy cadets were kibbutz members, or "kibbutzniks" in Hebrew.

A kibbutz is a communal settlement in Israel where members share all wealth and reinvest profits into the community. Kibbutz members ate and worked together in communal spaces. They promoted gender equality and created communal children's houses where kids learned, played, and slept together. This collective upbringing challenged the traditional family structure and allowed children to be less dependent on their parents. Kibbutz members seemed to skip the Self-Centric Potential and were 'born' into the Group-Centric Potential.

The kibbutzniks had a completely different background from mine. They shared everything. When they received weekly packages of goodies from their kibbutz, they shared them with everyone. In contrast, I kept the packages my parents sent me all to myself. I know—selfish prick. I feel uneasy admitting this.

Despite noticing my behavior, they included me fully and unconditionally. Though I couldn't initially understand their actions, I quickly adapted to their new ways. I owe my rapid transformation to the amazing kibbutzniks.

This is the key to transforming Self-Centric individuals. If they haven't changed on their own, they likely won't unless we, as a group, help them integrate into our community.

What is your transformation story? Can you recognize your change and still accept your Self-Centric self as part of your integrated identity?

Transforming to Group-Centric

I have no doubt that you're not Self-Centric, but you might want to help someone else transition to the Group-Centric Potential. The goal is to encourage this transformation by creating compelling external incentives that motivate change. Use the same fears, assumptions, safeguards, and beliefs that currently drive their behavior to guide them through the process.

Incentives and Motivation: Bonuses, commissions, and rewards for fitting into the group are effective strategies. Boost their motivation by making it clear that adaptation is not optional—it's mandatory. They must adapt or face failure. This approach taps into their fear of survival and fear of loss.

Role-Modeling and Social Skills: However, incentives alone aren't enough. We also need to role-model and help them develop basic social skills. Show them the benefits of shared goals and collective power. Help them understand that they are safer in a group than acting alone. Teach them how to rely on each other and how following social norms and group rules can both protect them and enhance their power.

The Bottom Line

Before moving to the next chapter, make sure you fully recognize the Self-Centric Potential within yourself. While very few adults remain at this stage, it's common for adolescents to experience it. Assisting others with this transformation helps complete our own integration and builds our empathy for the Self-Centric.

By understanding and facilitating this change, we can better support those around us and enhance our own growth and development.

CHAPTER 6.

FROM GROUP TO DOMAIN-CENTRIC

Grace, the VP of People Operations at the tech company, was taken aback by Damon's request for a one-on-one meeting. Damon, the VP of Integration, reported to the Chief Information Officer and was in charge of integrating all software platforms, including those related to human resources.

Damon wasted no time on pleasantries. He always seemed busy, constantly on the move. "I want you to lead the project for the new performance management system. This new AI platform will transform how we measure, track, and manage performance," he said, dropping a bombshell right from the start.

Grace felt her stress levels spike. "This is a technical project. I have no idea how to manage a technology project or lead the interface with all the business units. My team doesn't have the expertise," she replied, recalling the conflicts around previous platforms and dreading the possible upheaval. This was not a good time to rock the boat.

"Look, Damon, I really appreciate your suggestion, but my team is already working on various changes, and we don't have the time or resources to take on this project. Our plates are full," she said, almost out of breath.

"Yes, you do. You just got Stan a few months ago. I heard he's doing well. He's great with data. You're the only one who can understand the impact of the business requirements on performance management. If you don't agree, I will escalate this to my boss, and it will come to you from your boss," Damon responded firmly.

"No escalations, please," Grace said. "We don't work like this here."

"Look, Grace. You are not alone. I will work with you, and my team will work with your team. It's a collaborative project across the organization, but you must be the lead."

"Give me a few days to talk with my team. We make decisions together," Grace answered.

"Seriously? That slows things down. I don't have time. This isn't the only project we're running. What is there to talk about? I'll send the first project invite shortly. I've got to run. Bye." And off he went.

Grace realized she was on the edge of her capacity. Her Chief People Officer had recently remarked about the little impact she was making on the business, and that comment still echoed in her mind. She was scared of this new project. It put her in the limelight and, even worse, forced her into disagreements with leaders she had tried to avoid for a long time.

It was time for a change, but she didn't have a clue what or how to change.

Group-Centric Weaknesses

The strengths of any Centric Potential level diminish as we advance through each stage. When we fully realize our Potential at each level, what were once strengths start to become weaknesses. When these over-extended strengths begin to hinder us, it's time to let go and move to the next level.

By letting go, we're not discarding the strengths we've developed over the years; rather, we're opening ourselves up to new behaviors that align with the next-level Potential.

Stan moved beyond his Self-Centric weaknesses by adopting Grace's strengths. Now, Grace faces a new challenge: moving away from her Group-Centric strengths, which are becoming liabilities, and developing Domain-Centric strengths, which her company needs most from her.

The biggest liability of Group-Centric leaders is their tendency to relinquish power and conform to others' expectations in order to gain approval and feel secure. This constant need to meet expectations and please others can lead to feelings of helplessness and victimization.

People operating at the Group-Centric Potential face challenges in achieving high performance. Forming a vision, initiating strategy, and driving execution in organizations is difficult if you don't believe you can shape the future. As a result, those at the Group-Centric Potential often play it small, stay silent, avoid speaking up in meetings, and shy away from taking a stand in heated conversations.

In 360-degree assessments, colleagues frequently describe Group-Centric leaders as passive, non-assertive, self-doubting, overly cautious, and predictable. These leaders hold back their creative expression and avoid expressing disagreements. They seek approval and advice before taking action, let others make tough decisions, and wait for instructions.

Group-Centric leaders reach the edge of their capacity when their companies assign them responsibilities that demand high business performance, as they struggle to initiate and drive change.

Transformation into Domain-Centric leadership requires these leaders to stop identifying themselves solely through relationships and start relying on their expertise, experience, and mastery as their new, stronger voice.

By embracing this transformation, they can overcome the limitations of the Group-Centric Potential and step into roles that demand higher levels of performance and leadership.

Domain-Centric Strengths

Domain-Centric leaders no longer depend on or conform to others' opinions. They strive to excel in their profession and support their system, standing out for their unique expertise. They position themselves not just as experts but as true masters who are dedicated to doing the right thing.

Expertise and Mastery: Domain-Centric leaders are known for their deep knowledge and mastery of their craft. They take pride in their expertise and are committed to continuous improvement and excellence.

Self-Reliance: They are confident in their abilities and take charge of themselves. They do not seek external validation but are driven by their own standards of excellence.

Pragmatism and Data-Driven Approach: These leaders rely on science and data. They are highly pragmatic, making decisions based on facts and evidence. They are convinced by reasoning and logical arguments.

Analytical and Inquisitive: Domain-Centric leaders ask questions, gather facts, and seek to understand the reasons behind their actions. They constantly look for ways to improve accuracy, efficiency, processes, and procedures.

Leadership through Expertise: They lead by example, showcasing their mastery and setting high standards for others. Their expertise commands respect, and they inspire others through their dedication and competence.

Domain-Centric leaders excel in roles that demand specialized knowledge and the ability to drive improvements and innovations within their field.

Their strength lies in their unwavering commitment to their craft and their relentless pursuit of excellence.

Domain-Centric Recollection

After my rapid transformation into the Group-Centric Potential during the early days at the Air Force Flight Academy, the next five years were dedicated to becoming the best fighter pilot I could be. Hundreds of flights simulating combat and missions behind enemy lines helped me become a leader that wingmen could trust in battle.

My 20-year Air Force career was exciting and fulfilling. However, the years that followed were less thrilling. After graduating in economics with a minor in accounting, I moved into a career in corporate finance. As you can imagine, a career in corporate finance wasn't as exhilarating as being a fighter pilot.

Ironically, my lack of passion for finance turned out to be a blessing. I didn't stay in my Domain-Centric Potential for long and instead expanded my expertise into related areas of operations, which propelled me into the Vision-Centric Potential early in my corporate career.

However, I never completely let go of my Domain-Centric Potential. I continued to leverage my Domain-Centric skills as I transitioned into new professional areas.

Outgrowing our Self, Group, and Domain-Centric Potentials doesn't mean we stop using them. They remain integral parts of the Vision, Expansive, Integral, and Unitive Potentials.

What about you? Can you recall your transition from Group-Centric to Domain-Centric? Do you remember times when you operated at the Group-Centric Potential? Can you recall moments when you embodied the Domain-Centric Potential? Reflecting on these experiences helps us understand how each Potential has shaped our journey and continues to influence our growth.

Decide on the One Big Shift

The transformation from Group-Centric to Domain-Centric involves a shift in behavior, with specific actions that can be observed and recorded on video. The major behavior shifts to Domain-Centric include:

1. **Challenging Authority:** Questioning authority when there is a misalignment with your knowledge.
2. **Taking a Stand:** Taking a stand on professional issues and providing data to support your position.
3. **Expressing Needs and Wants:** Openly expressing what you want and need.
4. **Showing Personality:** Demonstrating your unique personality and voice based on your expertise and knowledge.
5. **Winning Arguments:** Winning arguments by being "right" through evidence and expertise.
6. **Professional Contribution:** Contributing to the group with professional mastery.
7. **Demonstrating Virtuosity:** Standing out by showcasing your virtuosity.

Each of these behavior shifts represents a significant challenge for Group-Centric leaders. Choose one behavior from the list that intrigues you and represents a notable change from your current Group-Centric behaviors. This will be your One Big Shift."

Identify Counter Behaviors

Two types of counter behaviors can hinder the shift into the Domain-Centric Potential: those we are currently engaging in and those we are not. As with earlier transitions, we express observable behaviors as verbs. Actions like thinking, reflecting, and noticing, which occur in our heads, are not considered behaviors. The common Group-Centric behaviors that hinder the transformation into Domain-Centric are:

Behaviors We Are Doing:

- Avoiding conflict
- Holding back creative expression
- Expressing disagreement only behind the back (passive-aggressive)
- Playing by the rules
- Acting to fit in
- Submitting my agenda to others' agendas
- Waiting for approvals to take actions

Behaviors We Are Not Doing:

- Not speaking when disagreeing
- Not initiating changes
- Not making decisions if not sure of management's position
- Not advocating opinions
- Not setting goals

Identifying these counter behaviors helps us connect to the fears that drive them.

Connect to Fears that Drive Counter Behaviors

The two main drivers of the Group-Centric Potential that hinder the transformation to Domain-Centric are conforming and seeking belonging. In contrast, Domain-Centric behaviors involve resisting conformity and stepping away from the need to belong. Domain-Centric leaders take a stand and engage in conflict.

When Group-Centric individuals try to adopt Domain-Centric behaviors, their fears may slow them down or completely halt their progress.

Here are some of the fears I've heard from executives trying to engage in more Domain-Centric behaviors:

- Being rejected, excluded, expelled, deserted, abandoned, cast out, exiled, avoided, ignored, or rejected
- Losing relationships
- Seen as non-collaborative, unfriendly, aggressive, or non-supportive

These fears don't go away on their own unless we understand the assumptions that cement these fears in our subconscious mind.

Construct Restraining Assumptions

As we did in the previous chapter, we identify the assumptions of each Potential by constructing "If, then" statements. For example, if I engage in X, Y, or Z Domain-Centric behaviors, then my worst Group-Centric fears will be realized. In other words, if I behave in a certain way, then I fear the worst consequences.

Let's examine some of the assumptions that prevent Group-Centric individuals from trying Domain-Centric behaviors. Note that these assumptions combine the behaviors and fears discussed earlier.

- If I challenge my manager, they will hold grudges against me.
- If I take a stand, they will reject me.
- If I say directly what I need, they will ignore me.
- If I demonstrate my unique personality and voice, I won't be part of the team anymore.
- If I win the argument and am "right," I'll lose the relationship.
- If I stand out by demonstrating virtuosity, they will exclude me in the future.

Reflect on your own experiences:

- What were your assumptions when you were at this Potential in the past?
- How did you invalidate these assumptions?

- What assumptions are you still making when you fall back to Group-Centric behaviors in the present?

By identifying and addressing these restraining assumptions, you can better understand the confining safeguards that hold you back in the Group-Centric Potential.

Release Confining Safeguards

Our subconscious mind creates safeguards to protect us from the uncomfortable emotions linked to our fears. These safeguards are part of the operating system that resists the changes we want to make. In any transformation, we need to address and unlock the five safeguards that resist change: identity, self-worth, footholds, equals, and rules.

Identity

For people who operate at the Group-Centric Potential, relationships generate a sense of identity:

- I'm my relationship.
- I'm my group, religion, or caste.
- I'm a proud member of...
- I'm nobody outside this group.
- I'm liked, loved, and accepted.

The transformation to Domain-Centric means that our identity is no longer tied to these relationships. Instead, we begin to develop a new identity based on our expertise, knowledge, experience, skills, and confidence in our best practices.

Self-Worth

In the Group-Centric Potential, self-worth grows as appreciation from others grows. The more appreciation we receive, the more we sacrifice for the group. You can often recognize a person at this Potential by their strong association with their group, which they may express through:

- I work for Google.
- I'm with the sales team.
- I graduated from Princeton.
- I played basketball with the Los Angeles Lakers.

Companies often tap into this Potential by creating a sense of belonging through in-house clubs for rewards and recognition, such as The President's Club or The High-Performance Club.

Footholds

Footholds are the mental anchors that hold people back at the Group-Centric Potential. Some common footholds include:

- I go along to get along.
- I don't want to rock the boat.
- I pick my battles.
- Loyalty protects me from disapproval.
- Shoulds, shouldn'ts, supposed to, ought to are signs of fear, obligation, and guilt: Stick to the rules.
- Us vs. them. They are not part of us.
- Our truth is the only truth.
- Our group is superior.
- I wanted to save face.
- We're a family here, and I'm a proud member.
- Loyalty is everything.

- Blood is thicker than water.
- Stronger together.

Pay attention when you hear phrases like these in your inner voice or in others' conversations, as they indicate the presence of Group-Centric Potential. People at this level often blame other groups for their problems and act inclusively only within their own groups. This 'us against them' mentality contributes to social divisiveness, which can be seen in politics, religious conflicts, and territorial disputes. It also plays a role in racism and discriminatory acts against minorities.

Equals

- Meeting expectations = success.
- Complying with my manager = safety.
- We win = I win.
- I am = what others think of me.
- Loyalty = respect our tradition.
- Hierarchy, status, money = better.
- Right way = diplomatic way.
- Criticism = they don't like me.
- Feedback = personal disapproval.

Group-Centric leaders are very sensitive to losing face and work hard to save face for themselves and others, hoping for reciprocity. "Save my face, and I will save your face. Scratch my back, and I'll scratch yours."

Rules

The Group-Centric Potential is driven by a tendency to create and follow rules. People at this level comply with existing rules and norms and often invent their own based on conditioning and submission to their primary group. They can fall into cultish behaviors and conspiracy theories about 'others,' operating under the belief that "this is how things should be," driven by fear.

While these rules can hinder the transformation to Domain-Centric Potential, they are a significant strength for professionals in roles that require strict adherence to procedures and rules, such as auditors, regulators, accountants, and quality controllers. It's important to recognize that someone may seem to operate at the Group-Centric Potential because of their job demands rather than their personal development stage. I experienced this early in my career as a financial controller, where colleagues in sales, marketing, and operations often saw me as bureaucratic and conservative simply based on my title.

Pair Beliefs with Interdependent Beliefs

The earlier the Potential, the stronger the beliefs. People operating from the Group-Centric Potential often have firmly held beliefs that are evident in their language. They use clichés, generalize with terms like 'always' and 'never,' rely on stereotypes, and employ superlatives.

Group-Centric individuals feel insecure and rely on others for security. Their need for certainty makes it difficult for them to handle complex and unpredictable situations.

Here are some common Group-Centric beliefs:

- Things should be in order.
- Things don't change.
- I shouldn't say what I think.
- Leaders know what they do.
- We need to win against them at all costs.
- If you are out of my group, you are an enemy.

- I need to fulfill others' expectations to succeed.
- Conflict is bad.
- I should always be nice.

Group-Centric individuals think in black and white, much like those at the Self-Centric level. This binary thinking and either-or judgments prevent them from recognizing, mapping, and leveraging polarities. They tend to identify with one side of a polarity while neglecting the other.

In the examples below, they prefer and depend on the left pole while neglecting the right pole that represents the new beliefs of the Domain-Centric Potential they are moving into:

- Pleasing others AND Expressing myself
- Generalizing AND Specifying
- Idealizing AND Realizing
- Tactful AND Candid
- Meeting others' expectations AND Setting my own expectations
- Loyal AND Objective
- Following norms AND Questioning norms
- Dependent AND Independent
- Positive AND Authentic
- Status AND Merit
- Conforming AND Questioning

Transformation doesn't mean we discard our current beliefs (left) and replace them with new beliefs (right). Instead, it involves leveraging the advantages of both sides of the polarities. Rather than relying solely on the left pole, we also incorporate the right pole, creating a more balanced perspective.

By recognizing and integrating these interdependent beliefs, we can move beyond binary thinking and adopt a more nuanced, flexible approach that fosters greater growth and adaptability.

Integrating Group-Centric for Transforming to Domain-Centric

I've worked with professionals in their forties and fifties who still struggle to complete their transformation to Domain-Centric. The difficulties they face are twofold:

Cultural Conditioning: Many executives have been culturally conditioned from an early age to be submissive to authority. For example, in some Asian cultures, respect and submission to power, authority, or age (such as parents, teachers, and elders) are strongly emphasized.

Fitting into Company Culture: Executives often try to fit into the company culture when they join a new employer. Even senior executives might hold back their observations to blend in with their new team. By the time they feel comfortable sharing their insights, they may be too entrenched in the culture to want to disrupt the status quo.

You may have already completed this transformation, but some people around you might not have completed their transformation, and you can help them make that shift.

The Group-Centric Potential exists within each of us, and we need to understand its role, develop deep compassion for it, and appreciate both its contributions and limitations. The better we integrate former Potentials into our sense of self and embrace the mosaic of Potentials that shape who we are, the faster we can evolve and help others evolve into higher Potentials.

Observing and Assisting:

- Start observing people around you. Do you see individuals who operate constantly from a Group-Centric Potential?
- Notice if people fall back to Group-Centric behaviors. Do you fall back from time to time?

By understanding and integrating these aspects, we can more effectively support others in their transformation. Helping others complete their shift from Group-Centric to Domain-Centric not only aids them but also enhances our own growth and development.

Developing compassion and recognizing the Group-Centric Potential within ourselves and others enables us to guide and support each other through these transformative processes. This ultimately fosters a more dynamic and evolved collective Potential.

Domain-Centric Transformations Moves

All transformations begin with small, safe experiments involving new behaviors associated with the next level—Domain-Centric. The key behavior for this Potential is the ability to challenge group thinking. Asking questions is the safest way to start making this shift.

Any thoughts and statements can be converted into inquiries. To help you frame these questions elegantly and effectively, use this simple 3-part framework:

1. **What I'm noticing** (seeing, hearing)
2. **What I'm feeling about what I'm noticing** (emotions, sensations)
3. **What's important for me** (my need/value)

Wrap it up with a question like, "Did I get it right?" or "Would you be willing to...?"

Use this framework not only to articulate what you notice, feel, and need for yourself but also to frame what the other person is noticing, feeling, and requesting. This can be challenging but rewarding.

Start Experimenting in a Safe Environment:

- Begin with family dinners or friends' parties, observing your own feelings and emotions and those of others. If you can't notice them, you can't express them.
- After practicing noticing emotions, try to express them in safe situations. Check if your fears about the response were confirmed and what this tells you about the assumptions, safeguards, and beliefs you built to protect yourself from fear.
- Observe people voicing different ideas and views. Can you find evidence for a small contrary view that you can offer to a group in a safe situation to test your assumptions?

Example of the Framework in Use:

- **Noticing:** "I'm noticing that during our team meetings, we often avoid discussing the challenges we face with the new project."
- **Feeling:** "I feel concerned because it seems like we might be missing out on addressing critical issues."
- **Importance:** "What's important to me is that we tackle these challenges head-on to ensure the project's success."
- **Question:** "Did I get it right? Would you be willing to discuss these challenges openly in our next meeting?"

Practicing with Others:

- **Noticing:** "I see that you've been working late frequently this week."
- **Feeling:** "I sense you might be feeling overwhelmed."
- **Importance:** "It's important to me that we support each other's well-being."
- **Question:** "Would you be willing to share what's been on your mind?"

By practicing this framework, you develop the ability to challenge group thinking in a constructive way. You learn to express your observations, emotions, and needs clearly and check your assumptions. Over time, this helps you grow into the Domain-Centric Potential and support others in their transformation journey as well.

Aaron Transformation Story

Aaron was a business analyst at a multinational tech company. In his early fifties, with two kids in college, he was tired of his back-office job and wanted a promotion. However, his 360-degree assessment revealed his leadership effectiveness was in the 13th percentile, with his passive tendencies nearing the 100th percentile. He scored high in complying, belonging, and conservatism, and felt his poor performance might cost him his job.

Despite these concerns, six months later, Aaron was promoted to Vice President, overseeing a customer-facing division with P&L responsibility. How did this happen?

Aaron set a Domain-Centric behavior change goal: to "address issues directly without smoothing them over." His biggest fear was being rejected and dismissed, which he felt would make him appear worthless.

He had assumed that addressing difficult issues (behavior) would lead to dismissal and being seen as worthless (fear). He realized he had built safeguards to protect his 'smart' identity and self-worth by avoiding conflict at all costs. His beliefs favored conforming over inquiring.

Changing these conforming behaviors was challenging. His subconscious commitment to never being dismissed, rejected, or seen as needy was obstructing his progress. His deeply held assumption was that addressing hard issues would lead to being perceived as unintelligent and unworthy, a notion unacceptable for a highly intelligent Stanford graduate.

Aaron began testing his assumptions by tackling tough conversations first at home with his college kids, then with his wife of 25 years, and eventually with friends. As he disconfirmed his assumptions, he gradually introduced these new behaviors into the boardroom.

Three months later, Aaron was promoted from Senior Director to Vice President, leading a business division with top and bottom-line responsibilities. A year later, he took the same 360-degree assessment again. Despite the challenges of his new role and team, his leadership effectiveness soared from the 13th percentile to the 78th percentile. His tendency to comply dropped from the 91st to the 12th percentile, and his performance scores increased from the 12th to the 66th percentile.

Emma's Transformation Story

Emma was the VP of Marketing at a biotech company. A mother of four girls in her late forties, Emma was considered a success. However, when she took a 360-degree assessment, her scores were high but not as high as she had expected, given her position and role in the senior leadership team.

She was particularly troubled by the low score she received for authenticity, which was in the 30th percentile. Additionally, her medium scores in Group-Centric tendencies—such as being passive, pleasing, belonging, and conservative—surprised her. She didn't see herself as someone who lacked the courage to have genuine conversations.

I had been coaching Emma for three years through various transformations, but this one was her first and most significant awakening. I suggested she perform a 'spouse test' to assess her Group-Centric tendencies with her husband. She was shocked by his feedback, which highlighted her risk-averse nature and its impact on their family. This was a significant issue they had never addressed before.

Motivated to change, Emma declared a new behavior change goal and shared it with her colleagues and family members. Her goal was to "address the elephants in the room," committing to discuss topics that no one else dared to address.

Following the 5-step transformation process, she identified her deepest fears: breaking relationships, facing retaliation, and disrupting the harmony in her senior leadership team, her marketing department, and her family relationships with her husband and teenage daughters. Once she was clear about her fears, she could see the assumptions she was subconsciously making:

- "If I address the elephants in the room, it will cause broken relationships."
- "If I address the elephants in the room, it will cause more trouble and friction, and I will lose support."

Emma realized she had subconsciously created safeguards to "protect" herself from breaking relationships and to preserve her identity as a 'team player,' as well as her self-worth, which was based on being a harmony maker. At the same time, she was stuck in a passive stance, convincing herself she was smart for "picking her battles."

She began to understand that her reliance on maintaining harmony had led her to neglect bold innovation. Emma started making small, safe experiments with new behaviors. Over the following 18 months, these efforts helped her transition from Group-Centric to Domain-Centric, and then from Domain-Centric to Vision-Centric.

A few months into her transformation, Emma was promoted to Senior VP, taking on responsibility for consolidating the clinical trials function. Eighteen months later, when she retook the 360-degree assessment, her authenticity score had more than doubled. I was impressed by how boldly she spoke in senior leadership team and board meetings, confronting group thinking and expressing her opinions with confidence.

Emma's journey demonstrates how addressing deeply rooted fears and assumptions can lead to significant personal and professional growth, transforming not only one's career but also relationships and self-perception.

What I Thought and What I Said

One of Emma's eye-opening exercises was reflecting on heated conversations and journaling two columns: one for 'What I Thought' and the other for 'What I Said.' The gaps between these columns revealed a lack of authenticity and integrity. The larger the gaps, the lower the authenticity and integrity, and vice versa. Try this exercise yourself to discover how authentic you really are.

'Carefrontation'

Another framework that helped Emma make a transformative change was leveraging the Caring AND Confronting polarity. In this framework, Caring represents the Group-Centric preference, while Confronting represents the Domain-Centric behavior that was previously neglected. This framework provides an effective conversation starting point following a 7-step process that must be completed in 60 seconds or less:

1. **Name the issue:** "I want to talk with you about the effect *(contribution)* is having on **(impact)**."
2. **Select a specific example** that illustrates the behavior or situation you want to change: "For example, _____."
3. **Describe your emotion** around the issue (not what you're thinking): "I feel _____." (e.g., frustrated, disturbed, disappointed, etc.)
4. **Clarify why this is important:** What is at stake? "From my perspective, the stakes are high. _____ is at stake."

5. **Apologize for your contribution(s)** to this problem even if you haven't contributed. This prevents defensiveness: "I should have brought this up earlier. I recognize my fingerprints. I have/may have ____. For this, I apologize."

6. **Indicate your wish to resolve this issue:** Exactly the issue you mentioned, not the example. The real issue: "I want to resolve this with you (restate the issue)."

7. **Invite your partner to respond:** "I sincerely want to understand your perspective. Talk to me."

To illustrate the framework, let's look at a tough conversation a CEO at a B2B enterprise software company has with the CRO about business results falling short of the quarter target.

"Hey Bill, I want to talk with you about the impact transactional relationships with our customers have on our ability to develop long-term partnerships with them. I read the summary of the meetings your team had with customer XYZ that ended without sales and noticed that most of the time was spent on the contract terms, with little conversation on the future value for their customers. I'm very disappointed that our relationship value wasn't embodied in these negotiations. Relational rather than transactional is the DNA of our company culture. Transactional conversations deviate from this culture. I apologize for not discussing it with you before the quarter's end. I want to resolve the issue of the transactional relationships with our customers. I'm curious. What's your point of view?"

Less than 60 seconds. Right? Have you noticed how this opening is:

- Powerful AND respectful
- Direct AND empathetic
- Bold AND sensitive
- Confronting AND caring

The Bottom Line

Aaron and Emma weren't fully at the Group-Centric Potential when they started their transformations, and neither are you. Their behaviors were residual fallback tendencies that hadn't been completely integrated or transformed, despite their extensive experience and mid-life status.

They wouldn't have had the chance to continue evolving if they hadn't addressed and transformed the Group-Centric behaviors they still defaulted to under pressure. They are not unique cases. I've worked with many leaders who still default to Group-Centric behaviors under pressure. We all do, to varying extents, until we become fully aware of these tendencies.

Over years of working with leaders, nearly everyone has successfully completed their transformation using the framework described in this book. Those who struggled to release their footholds despite their efforts often had underlying issues that required therapy.

Although only 10% of leaders may have Group-Centric as their dominant Potential, this mindset affects all of us to some degree. Falling back on these behaviors can slow our future development.

Now, let's explore the integration and transformation from Domain-Centric to Vision-Centric—a challenging transition—and understand how the Domain-Centric Potential can obstruct this process.

CHAPTER 7.

FROM DOMAIN TO VISION-CENTRIC

Leaders who transform from Domain-Centric to Vision-Centric derive their identity and self-worth from within (inside-out), unlike those in earlier Potentials who rely on the group, profession, bosses, family, or community (outside-in).

Vision-Centric leaders are not swayed by other people's agendas. They effectively drive their own vision within their organizations and beyond. Having freed themselves from dependency on others' affirmations, they are willing to take risks in setting their own direction and moving toward it.

Damon's Story

Damon, the Integration VP, was upset after reading an email from Expi, the CEO. Expi wrote that the executive team had been working with a Potential development coach for a year and decided to expand the program to second-tier leaders, including Damon.

"I have no time for this B.S.," thought Damon. "I'm already swamped with projects and tight deadlines. How can I fit this into my schedule?"

He immediately walked into his boss' office and asked to be taken off the program. Vision, the Chief Information Officer, listened to Damon's ranting, letting him vent his frustration and list his to-dos. Damon always reminded her how busy he was.

"Damon, you're frustrated about the Potential development program, worried it will disrupt your project deadlines, and it seems you're not focused on your growth and future promotions. Did I get that right?"

Damon was stunned. Vision noticed the sweat on his forehead. "Eh...no. I didn't say that. Of course, I want a promotion. But how will I be promoted if I don't deliver on time?"

"So, you're confused about how the program will help you deliver on time, and it seems you prioritize efficiency over the impact of your projects. Is that right?" asked Vision.

"No. For me, efficiency and effectiveness are the same. If I'm not delivering on time, I'm ineffective," replied Damon.

"And if you deliver on time but complete an unnecessary project perfectly, you're a super-efficient but ineffective leader, Damon. You're doing a great job executing other stakeholders' requirements, but that's not enough for the next level. You're stuck. This program will help you get unstuck."

Damon left Vision's office, surprised by her response. He always considered himself a rising technology star, and the idea of being stuck shocked him.

Two weeks later, his direct reports, peers, Vision, Expi, and others across the company completed his 360-degree Potential assessment. The debrief with his coach was a wake-up call.

The 360-degree assessment revealed that his colleagues saw him as highly controlling and critical. He scored high on perfectionism and autocratic behaviors, and his performance scores were surprisingly low.

"How is this possible when I'm doing a great job and am the best in my domain of expertise?" he asked his coach.

"It's a leadership Potential assessment, Damon, not a technology assessment," the coach replied. "Your low scores in collaboration, teamwork, and relationships explain your leadership challenges. Leadership is a people game."

Domain-Centric Weaknesses

In the previous chapter, we highlighted the impressive strengths of the Domain-Centric Potential. This Potential represents experts who excel in their fields—scientists, surgeons, professors, pilots, astronauts, lawyers, accountants, and many others. However, these strengths can also become weaknesses that hinder their ability to scale their influence, much like Damon's experience.

35% of all leaders in our database are stuck in the Domain-Centric Potential, willingly or unwillingly. This is the largest percentage of any Potential. This wouldn't be a problem if all these leaders were individual contributors working independently. However, many of these leaders manage teams, collaborate with cross-functional groups, and report to senior leaders. They struggle in their interactions with stakeholders—upward (bosses), downward (direct reports), and laterally (peers).

Single Point of View: Domain-Centric leaders immerse themselves so deeply in their craft that they see it as the only way of thinking. To others, these leaders may seem dogmatic, reactive, and argumentative.

Stuck in the Details: They tend to get bogged down in details because they rely heavily on data they consider "undisputed facts."

Perfectionist: They set such high standards that almost nothing meets their expectations. As a result, they are highly critical, competitive, and unreceptive to feedback.

Know-It-All: When engaging with Domain-Centric leaders for an extended period, you may sense a degree of superiority. They always seem to have an answer and rarely appear to be at a loss.

Defensive: These leaders are less aware of their feelings and shortcomings. They brush off criticism and always try to be "right," often arguing their point of view for hours.

Domain-Centric leaders often struggle to view issues from perspectives outside their domain expertise and have difficulty merging opposites into holistic, co-creative solutions. This limitation can lead them to hit their capacity edge, feeling a burning need to advance to the Vision-Centric level.

Vision-Centric Strengths

The Vision-Centric Potential is the driving force behind organizations. Leaders operating at this level focus on the results and outcomes of their organizations.

Cross-Functional Collaboration: Vision-Centric leaders value interdisciplinary teams and strive for win-win solutions that create alignment within and beyond their teams. They are collaborative and pragmatic, favoring "good enough" over perfection.

Confidence and Certainty: These leaders exude confidence and a positive, can-do attitude. They often operate with a sense of certainty, sometimes based on the incorrect assumption that they control the context necessary to support their vision, goals, and results.

Result-Driven: Vision-Centric leaders excel in delivering results, particularly in the short term, by focusing their teams on prioritized goals. They actively seek feedback to help them achieve their goals, learn, improve, and fulfill their Potential.

Effective Delegation: They are skilled in delegating tasks, coaching their teams, and intuitively adjusting the team's pace for success. However, they may struggle to maintain a work-life balance.

Bill Torbert, professor emeritus at Boston College and author of *Action Inquiry*, refers to this Potential as the Achiever. The Achiever takes responsibility for personal and team actions, manages demands within time constraints, evaluates and improves ideas across functions, values teamwork and ethics, communicates well with senior management, and appreciates relationships.

Domain to Vision-Centric Recollection

I made a significant career mistake by choosing the wrong profession. This error was part of a multi-decade chain of missteps that began in high school when I opted for math and science—subjects I was good at—over liberal arts, which was my true passion. Despite my interest in liberal arts, I was advised by teachers, parents, and friends that following my heart would lead to financial instability.

The pattern continued in college. I graduated with a degree in economics and accounting and joined a CPA firm to earn my license. Just three months into my two-year practice, I told the senior partner, "I'm done! This isn't for me." Rather than letting me go, he transferred me to the management consulting division, which was a better fit.

A few years later, I joined Hadera Paper as their financial controller, despite my lack of enthusiasm for finance. Unlike my predecessor, who spent all day in the office handling paperwork, I focused on my true passion—operations. I dedicated myself to understanding every aspect of the site, which was as large as a small town and had its own power plant and wastewater treatment facility.

By immersing myself in operations and maintaining my role as financial controller, I gained a unique perspective that no one else had—a broad, functional viewpoint. Within a year, after years of losses, the company turned profitable due to improved efficiencies. This success was possible because I didn't limit myself to my domain expertise. I developed a vision for the organization despite resistance and people questioning my "professionalism."

What about you? Have you moved beyond your functional profession to embrace a purpose, vision, and goals that impact the organization beyond your domain expertise? If not, the next steps will guide you through this transformation.

Decide on the One Big Shift

Many believe that transformation is solely an inner process. While it is true that inner change is crucial, it's not enough on its own. The real measure of transformation is how it manifests in observable behaviors, as noticed by those around us. We shift from Domain-Centric to Vision-Centric by adopting specific Vision-Centric behaviors. Here are some key behaviors to consider for your One Big Shift:

Focusing on Outcomes: Vision-Centric leaders prioritize results over processes. They emphasize effectiveness over efficiency, opting for a pragmatic approach to achieving goals and making an impact.

Collaborating Across Functions: Vision-Centric leaders work well with interdisciplinary teams and professionals from different fields, valuing diverse perspectives.

Speaking Directly at Issues: They address issues head-on, express their core values, and act decisively, even in high-stakes situations.

Giving and Asking for Feedback: They provide direct, honest feedback and actively seek feedback from others, using it to improve.

Asking Questions: They replace statements with questions. They inquire as much as they advocate, asking questions like: "How is that for you?" "How did you come to see it that way?" "What if you couldn't do it anymore?" "When do you take responsibility for what is not your responsibility?"

Facilitating Conversations: Instead of controlling conversations, they focus on facilitating them.

Delegating: They effectively delegate tasks, using others as an extension of themselves to achieve goals.

Reflecting: They make time for self-reflection and observe themselves from an external perspective.

Initiating and Innovating: They challenge the status quo and drive change with relentless determination.

Seeking Consensus: They engage in mutual, equal relationships, accepting disagreements and moving forward collaboratively.

Driving Teamwork: They foster a sense of camaraderie, align the team around a shared purpose, coordinate tasks, and define the expected team culture and behaviors.

Taking Responsibility: They fully own their actions, particularly when things go wrong, and take responsibility for their team's mistakes.

A CEO I coached described his Vision-Centric Potential as a GPS that identifies the location and set direction using three 'satellites':

1. **Business** - vision, strategy, decisions, execution, and results.
2. **Relationships** - interpersonal intelligence, teamwork, collaboration, and connection).
3. **Being** - Courageous authenticity and integrity.

By focusing on one of these Vision-Centric behaviors as your One Big Shift, you can begin to transform your leadership style and influence, making your growth both visible and impactful.

Identify Counter Behaviors

The Domain-Centric behaviors leaders adopted during the shift from Group-Centric Potential become obstacles once they fully realize the Domain-Centric Potential. What were once strengths turn into weaknesses as leaders aim to grow into the Vision-Centric Potential. Let's examine some of these behaviors:

- Arguing endlessly about my position.
- Jumping to solve problems without paying attention to what people are experiencing.
- Insisting on doing things my way ("My way or the highway").
- Getting too much into the weeds and stuck in the details.
- Criticizing other people's work.
- Defending my position furiously.
- Attempting to "win" arguments.
- Counting solely on data to prove my points.
- Expecting others to show a similar commitment to professionalism as I do.
- Operating independently because it's more efficient.

- Not accepting "good enough" work unless it's perfect.
- Not admitting my mistakes and shortcomings.
- Not expressing emotions and feelings.
- Not asking for help when I'm stuck.
- Not accepting feedback. Getting defensive.
- Not delegating when too much is at stake.
- Not listening well to other people's points of view.

This list is extensive, and not all behaviors will apply to everyone. Are there specific counterproductive behaviors that still impede your progress? Reflect on the behaviors you have changed in the past. How did you achieve those changes?

By identifying these counterproductive behaviors, you can better understand which ones might be preventing you from reaching the Vision-Centric Potential.

Connect to Fears that Drive Counter Behaviors

People at the Domain-Centric Potential often fear becoming part of the herd again—unseen and unrecognized, as they were when they were Group-Centric. To uncover these fears, consider the worst-case scenarios that arise when you engage in behaviors contrary to those typical of the Domain-Centric Potential.

For example, one behavior on the list is "Arguing endlessly about my position." What is the fear if you don't argue your position? For me, it is being "seen as unknowledgeable," or "seen as incompetent."

Here are some fears driving the other behaviors:

- Being undistinguished
- Being wrong

- Being unprofessional
- Not being as good as others
- Having no answers
- Seen as weak
- Not being good enough
- Making mistakes
- Being inefficient
- Failing to execute
- Not performing up to expectations

You can group the fears into two types:

1. **Intellect:** Fears related to intellect—being worthy, smart, accomplished, knowledgeable, and expert.
2. **Performance:** Fears related to performance—getting things done the right way and executing tasks and projects in a timely manner.

Reflect on Your Fears:

- What are your fears?
- What were your fears in the past?
- Do they come back from time to time?

Construct Restraining Assumptions

Following the same two fear groups, there are primarily two assumption groups: those related to intellect and those related to performance.

Intellect Assumptions:

- For me to be right, others have to be wrong, and vice versa.
- I'm worthy if I'm right, so I need to find the weaknesses in others.
- I'm valuable because of my competencies, capabilities, and insights.
- I need to win over others to feel good about myself.

Performance Assumptions:

- Anything less than perfect is not acceptable.
- Failure will lead to my demise.
- I'm a loser if I don't win.

We identify more assumptions by combining the behaviors and the fears in 'if (behavior), then (fear).' Here are some examples:

- If I'm undistinguished, I'll lose my seat at the table.
- If I don't argue my position, I'll be proven wrong.
- If I don't jump to solve the problem, somebody else will solve it.
- If I don't insist on doing things my way, I'm undistinguished.
- If I'm not in the details, I'll be seen as unprofessional.
- If I admit mistakes, I'm not good enough.
- If I delegate, I'll fail to execute.
- If I ask for help, I'll be seen as weak.
- If I accept feedback, I'm not as good as the others.
- If I show emotions, I'm unprofessional.

There are endless variations of behaviors and fears that generate endless assumptions. We are all different, and we have different assumptions that configure our operating systems.

Reflect on Your Assumptions:

- What assumptions did you hold in the past?
- Do you still hold some of them?
- How have you disconfirmed these assumptions?

Release Confining Safeguards

Our subconscious mind believes our assumptions are true. Therefore, it establishes safeguards to protect us from the bad things that might happen if these assumptions are true.

Domain-Centric Identity

Domain-Centric leaders often define themselves by their profession and main craft, making "what I do" a central part of their identity. When you meet a Domain-Centric leader, they are quick to tell you their role—whether they are engineers, AI experts, management consultants, investment bankers, or lawyers. What they mean is:

- I'm my profession ("I'm a doctor")
- I'm an expert (I'm a surgeon")
- I'm special (I'm an ex-Googler)

For instance, I coached several senior legal advisors aiming to become Chief Legal Officers. To secure a C-suite position, they needed to shift to a Vision-Centric Potential and expand their focus to encompass all business aspects. However, after decades of operating at the Domain-Centric level, they were so ingrained in debating and winning arguments that they struggled to imagine changing. Their identity was firmly rooted in the legal profession, where they believed there was always one right answer and one wrong, and they could never be on the wrong side. They complained about their bosses being "too political" and "too compromising" their legal position when "pushed" by business executives.

Reflect on your own identity. How do you introduce yourself? Is your identity tied to your profession?

Domain-Centric Self-worth

Domain-Centric leaders establish their self-worth by being right all the time. They feel worthy by comparing themselves to others and perfecting their craft.

- I'm worthy when I win an argument
- I'm worthy when I'm right

- I'm worthy when the other is wrong
- I'm worthy when I'm perfect
- I'm worthy when I stand out from the crowd
- I'm worthy when I'm the best
- I'm worthy when I'm in control
- I'm worthy when I personally contribute
- I'm worthy when I solve problems and fix bugs
- I'm worthy when others come to ask my advice

Think about what makes you feel worthy. Do you derive self-worth from your profession, expertise, and knowledge?

Domain-Centric Footholds

Domain-Centric leaders typically reply to "How're you doing?" with "I'm very busy." They constantly struggle with time management and feel perpetually busy because they aim for perfection and high efficiency. These conflicting goals leave them stressed, burned out, and lacking work-life balance. They strive to end each day with "nothing in my inbox or on my desk."

The core challenge for Domain-Centric leaders is their belief in a single, logical truth, which they expect to be explainable through data, and if that fails, through authority and power. This belief in one truth can be a major obstacle, as it ties them to their established footholds and makes it difficult to adapt.

- Knowledge is power—the more I know, the more powerful I am
- Never being seen as less than competent
- Never not being in control of facts
- Never losing status
- Never being seen as vulnerable or weak
- Always being certain and having the right answer
- Not knowing or making mistakes is unacceptable

- If things don't go according to plan, find who and what's responsible
- Get the best practices and standards right

What footholds still hold you back? Have you noticed any of these footholds playing a role in your life? How do others experience you?

Domain-Centric Equals

We often aren't aware of the equations our subconscious mind creates. These deeply ingrained equations subtly influence our behaviors without us noticing. I sometimes record coaching sessions, transcribe them, and review the transcripts with my clients.

While reviewing a transcript with the COO of a tech company, he experienced an "aha" moment. He realized that when people disagreed with him, he didn't trust them. This insight was not immediately obvious. During our discussion, he described a situation where he had a major disagreement and then mentioned another instance where he didn't trust the person he had disagreed with. This realization was a huge blind spot for him. Once this issue was brought to light, he was able to shift to the Vision-Centric Potential, overcoming a decade of stagnation in the Domain-Centric role as COO without fully performing in the position.

A few other typical equals that get in the way are:

- Knowledge = Trust
- Feedback = Criticism = Not good enough
- Effective = Efficient
- Truth = Data
- Performance = Expertise

What are the equals that hold you back? Can you think of equals that held you back in the past? Are you able to spot other people's equals when they speak with you? How can you discuss what you are noticing with them?

Domain-Centric Rules

Unlike Group-Centric leaders, who adhere to group norms, Domain-Centric leaders follow rigid professional rules. For instance, some CFOs I've worked with were inflexible about accounting or treasury principles. This rigidity often led to conflicts with peers over budgets, disagreements with CEOs about investments, and challenges with spouses over parenting decisions.

Common rules include:

- Strictly following procedures
- Always gathering data
- Learning what you don't know
- Doing things the "right way"
- Believing "good enough" is not good enough
- Preferring best practices as the safest option
- Viewing exceptions as dangerous
- Prioritizing tangibles over intangibles
- Insisting "We need evidence"
- Believing "The truth is..."

Do any of these rules resonate with you? Do they still have a little voice in your head? Do you notice these rules in how your colleagues express themselves?

Pair Beliefs with Interdependent Beliefs

Domain-Centric leaders thrive in predictable environments but often struggle in unpredictable situations. They believe every problem has a solution and focus on finding the best one. This mindset can lead to rigidity, especially in complex scenarios that require innovative approaches.

Their core belief is that embracing ambiguity risks losing certainty, leading them to "force" best practices even when novel solutions are needed.

133

While Group-Centric leaders frequently use terms like "should," "must," and "would," Domain-Centric leaders often use "but," "nevertheless," and "however" in conversations, signaling their tendency to argue. They commonly struggle to see interdependent perspectives and find it difficult to leverage polarities.

Here are some polarities where Domain-Centric leaders lean heavily on the left pole, neglecting the right. Transforming to Vision-Centric requires leveraging both sides:

- Tangible AND Intangible
- Quantitative data AND Qualitative data
- Doing things right AND Doing the right things
- Efficiency AND Effectiveness
- Advocating AND Inquiring
- Directing AND Collaborating
- Being right AND Being aligned
- Details AND Big Picture
- Perfecting AND Delivering

Do you leverage equally both poles of these polarities? Do you still rely more on the left side? Are there other polarities of values, competencies, or beliefs you notice?

Transforming to Vision-Centric
Expansiveness

Leaders with a center of gravity in the Domain-Centric Potential are exceptional learners and knowledge seekers. Many are highly ambitious, aspiring to lead large teams and climb the corporate ladder, though some may not share this ambition. Leveraging this strength helps them transform quickly, as the desire to scale requires expanding their knowledge beyond their domain expertise.

Expanding into multiple domains, where they may never become true experts, necessitates collaboration with peers and learning from individuals with diverse educational backgrounds and perspectives. This approach supports a rapid transition to Vision-Centric leadership.

For example, a COO I worked with was initially quiet in meetings when the Chief Revenue Officer presented revenue-generating ideas. He said, "I don't know enough about sales to participate. He is a sales expert. I trust him." This reflects the Domain-Centric belief that everyone should work within their area of expertise.

Such a mindset often leads to a siloed culture. However, business growth involves more than just sales; it encompasses product development, service excellence, and customer-facing innovation, all of which require cross-functional collaboration. The COO became highly effective on the senior leadership team once he embraced the Vision-Centric Potential, actively engaging in discussions that spanned multiple domains.

Find Your WHY

The second strategy for transforming from Domain-Centric to Vision-Centric is developing a purposeful vision. This vision is highly inspiring when it is rooted in a clear sense of 'why I'm doing what I'm doing.' Even leaders who already operate at the Vision-Centric level but lack clarity about their driving force will struggle to fully immerse in this Potential.

In *Find Your WHY*, Simon Sinek outlines a simple process for discovering your purpose. He suggests that our WHY already exists within us and can be uncovered by examining the highlights and lowlights of our lives. Sharing these stories with a coach or a skilled listener can help reveal patterns of 'contribution' and 'impact' that might not be immediately obvious.

Contribution refers to the profound value you bring to the world—what genius you've leveraged throughout your life, both personally and professionally.

Impact is the effect your contribution has had on others, both directly and indirectly.

By identifying themes in your stories, you can distinguish between contributions and impacts. This leads to creating a purpose statement in two parts:

"To (contribution), so that together we (impact)."

For example, my purpose is "to augment leadership Potential so that together we create a ripple effect of unity in our divided world." This purpose inspires me every day and is the reason for writing this book.

A powerful purpose statement can counteract fears that lead to assumptions, which in turn require safeguards to protect beliefs. The stronger our purpose, the fewer fears will drive counterproductive behaviors.

Emma, the Vice President of Marketing at a biotech company, quickly transitioned from Domain-Centric to Vision-Centric after discovering her 'why.' By sharing her high and lowlight stories, she uncovered her WHY:

- **Contribution:** Develop entrepreneurial teams to grow and help patients
- **Impact:** So that together, we live happier lives.

Here are some purpose statements from my clients that helped them transition to Vision-Centric Potential and beyond:

- Build equitable culture so that together, we become our best selves.
- Develop high-performance teams so that together, we create a ripple effect of growth for everyone we reach.

- Connect people into high-performing teams so that together, we create freedom of choice.
- Create emotional experiences so that together, we build a caring culture in our family (organization).
- Mobilize resources and solve problems so that together, we create alignment and trust in the world.

Clarify Your Vision

Vision-Centric leaders have a vision that is deeply rooted in purpose. While purpose is long-term and aspirational, vision focuses on a 3-5 year horizon. It vividly illustrates how pursuing your purpose will manifest in the near future.

A powerful 'why,' combined with a purposeful vision, generates energy not only for you but also for everyone around you. People are drawn not just to what you do but to why you do it. Your purposeful vision will inspire others to join you, especially when it resonates with their hearts and minds.

For example, my vision is to help leadership teams augment their Potential to become super-effective in hyper-complexity. This vision appears prominently in my profiles, bios, and media introductions. It clearly extends from my purpose, which I share publicly at every opportunity. It outlines my focus for the next 5-10 years on evolving Potential so that my clients can create positive changes for both internal and external stakeholders, including society and the environment.

Establish Your Values

Corry, a Vice President of Sales at a multinational tech company, was shocked to discover that her integrity scores were low in a 360-degree assessment. "How is it possible?" she asked, as she saw herself as having high integrity but realized others did not perceive it the same way.

Integrity means walking your talk. Low integrity can stem from either not sharing your values or not living them consistently. Your values represent what you care about and stand for.

Corry knew her values but thought they were too personal to share. She is right. Values are personal, and so is leadership. If you're unsure about your top three values that everyone should know, take a moment to reflect and write them down.

My three values are unity (encompassing equality, justice, and freedom), courage (encompassing authenticity, vulnerability, and integrity), and empathy (encompassing presence, listening, and love). These guide my relationships with clients, colleagues, friends, and family.

But here's a caveat: a value becomes genuine only when you are willing to pay the price for it. Until then, it's just empty words. For instance, the courage to tell the truth to my coaching clients has sometimes cost me clients who did not want to hear it. Expressing empathy with Palestinians and promoting unity between Palestinians and Israelis has cost me relationships with Israeli family members who valued loyalty to the group more than universal unity.

From my clients, I often hear that their companies claim "employees are our most important assets" yet conduct massive layoffs at the first sign of trouble. This reveals their so-called values as mere public relations.

Articulating your 'why,' vision, and values—and living by them—creates a strong sense of integrity with those you work and live with. Now, it's your turn to articulate your purpose, vision, and three values succinctly and powerfully.

Ask, Receive, and Give Feedback

A major difference between Vision-Centric leaders and those at earlier Potentials is their willingness to ask for feedback—a lot of it. Leaders at the Self, Group, and Domain-Centric levels rarely seek feedback.

Asking for feedback is challenging because we never know what we'll hear. Inviting constructive criticism makes the process even tougher. Surprisingly, asking for feedback can sometimes make others uncomfortable, depending on the relationship. For example, when I ask my wife for feedback, she often says, "It's all great." I believe there's always room for improvement, so I press further, recognizing that it's difficult to give honest feedback to a partner when there's so much at stake.

The effectiveness of asking for feedback also hinges on power dynamics. Direct reports are less likely to provide direct feedback to their bosses due to fear of repercussions. Therefore, anonymous surveys and assessments can be more effective for uncovering our strengths and weaknesses. This approach helps foster a culture of giving and receiving feedback within organizations, families, and communities, where feedback flows freely among everyone.

When you receive feedback, the best response is, "Thank you. I'll reflect on this and get back to you." This is the Vision-Centric leaders' approach. In contrast, Domain-Centric leaders often respond defensively, offering explanations rather than considering the feedback.

Providing unsolicited feedback requires sensitivity, even when your relationship with the recipient seemingly grants you the "authority" to offer feedback, be it a direct report, partner, or child. Early Potentials view feedback as an unwelcome intrusion or personal attack akin to trespassing. To avoid this, ask for permission beforehand: "May I offer you some feedback?" This approach fosters receptiveness and encourages individuals to embrace your insights openly.

Establishing a culture of actively seeking, receiving, and providing feedback fosters psychological safety within organizations and families. This environment promotes feedback-seeking attitudes when doing performance reviews, advocating for innovative ideas, and experimenting with fresh approaches. Embracing feedback yields valuable insights for driving transformative changes that propel us toward realizing our Vision-Centric Potential.

Convert Statements into Questions

Inquiring is the new modus operandi for Vision-Centric leaders. This shift from making Domain-Centric *statements* to asking Vision-Centric *questions* represents a change from being righteous to being curious. Openness replaces distance.

Inquiry is both a process and a mindset. It helps identify blind spots but doesn't come naturally to Domain-Centric leaders making the transition to Vision-Centric Potential. They need to consciously convert statements into questions until it becomes second nature.

Fortunately, we encounter many daily situations where we can practice this shift. In both our personal and professional lives, we often make statements that can be reframed as inquiries. For example, when my daughter Avery went through adolescence, our relationship became strained. My attempts to enforce what I believed was best for her came across as controlling, especially as she was developing her independence. When I began converting my statements into questions, our relationship improved quickly and dramatically. I experienced a similar shift with my peers and board members. Our personal and professional lives are intertwined, and changes in one area often affect the other.

Now it's your turn to practice converting statements into questions. For example:

From Domain to Vision-Centric

- "You need to reduce inventory!" becomes "What will be the impact of reducing inventory?"
- "You can't go with your friends before finishing your homework!" becomes "What are the consequences of going with your friends without doing your homework?"

By consistently practicing this shift, you can enhance your leadership effectiveness and foster a more collaborative and open environment.

Reflect Consistently

The key difference between Vision-Centric leaders and their Self, Group, and Domain-Centric predecessors is their ability to observe and reflect on their own behaviors. Earlier Potentials lack this crucial skill.

Reflection begins by setting aside a few minutes each day to pause and ask yourself a few key questions:

- What worked well today?
- What didn't work well today?
- What do I want to change?

That's it. Reflection might sound complex, but it's simply about taking a moment to evaluate your day. Most leaders skip this step, which is why they often feel stuck. Spending just five minutes a day on reflection is transformative—no exaggeration.

The process is straightforward: Reflect, plan, act, observe, and repeat.

In the following chapters you'll learn to shorten the time between reflecting, planning, acting, and observing. Eventually, you'll be able to reflect on situations in real-time rather than only conducting postmortem analyses.

141

The Bottom Line

The transformation from Domain-Centric Potential, which encompasses 35% of leaders, to Vision-Centric Potential, representing 30% of leaders, is challenging but immensely rewarding. Vision-Centric leaders are highly valued and rewarded within organizations. Those who make this shift often find numerous opportunities for promotions.

In Part 3, we will delve into the Transformer Potentials. These Potentials focus on integrating and transcending previous stages, allowing you to navigate complexity with ease and inspire transformation in others. Prepare to explore the advanced stages of leadership Potential and discover how to become a truly transformative leader.

PART 3
TRANSFORMER POTENTIAL TRANSFORMATIONS

CHAPTER 8.

FROM VISION-CENTRIC TO EXPANSIVE TRANSFORMER

The transformation from Vision-Centric to Expansive Transformer isn't just another change; it's a meta-change that only 15% of leaders make. Vision-Centric leaders are highly effective, but as they scale to the C-suite or move into more complex industries, they often reach the limits of their Potential and begin to lose their effectiveness.

The 21st century has brought increasing levels of 'volatility,' 'uncertainty,' 'complexity,' and 'ambiguity' (VUCA), along with a world that is increasingly 'brittle,' 'anxious,' 'nonlinear,' and 'incomprehensible' (BANI). The higher the VUCA and BANI, the less effective Centric Potentials become.

Artificial Intelligence (AI) disrupts even the most sophisticated industries, not to mention traditional ones. Therefore, CEOs of high-growth or global companies should aspire to become Integral Transformers.

Integral is the destination; Expansive is just a pit stop.

As you expand your capacity, you continue to leverage your Vision-Centric strengths, which are primarily outcome-oriented. However, as you grow into the Expansive Potential, you let go of your attachment to goals and the belief that you control outcomes. This is difficult in a world that assesses performance and success based on outcomes.

The Expansive Transformer leverages both tangible and intangible outcomes, which Centric Potentials can't fully comprehend. The transformation from Vision-Centric to Expansive Transformer involves moving from the conventional to the unconventional, from knowledge to wisdom, and from independence to interdependence.

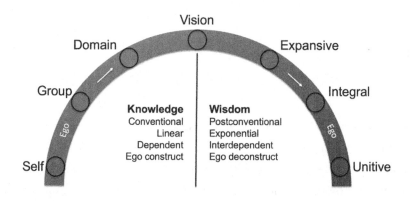

Figure 8.1 – From Knowledge to Wisdom

Letting go of the ego that we have worked so hard to build is the most challenging part of this transformation.

The Journey Ahead

In the following sections, we'll delve into the advanced stages of leadership Potential. This journey starts with the Expansive Transformer Potential, integrating and transcending previous Potentials to navigate complexity with ease and inspire transformation in others.

From here on, the path becomes fuzzy. That's why only 15% of leaders become Transformers. The transformation to Expansive Potential is possible if you have fully completed your transition to Vision-Centric. If you find the next chapters challenging to comprehend, it might indicate that you haven't yet fully integrated and transformed. Take the time to do the work, and revisit this material when you're ready.

This book isn't meant to be a one-sitting page-turner. It's designed to guide your life journey over multiple years or even decades.

Prepare to delve deeper into the complexities of becoming an Integral Transformer and discover how to navigate and inspire transformation in an increasingly complex world. Your journey continues here, step by step, as you evolve into a truly transformative leader.

Vision Story

Expi, the CEO of the tech company mentioned earlier, was having lunch with Vision, the Chief Information Officer, when he broke the news.

"The CTO is leaving to launch their own startup. I want you to replace them," Expi said. "You've done a fantastic job building high-performing teams and platforms that run our business, and I believe you can replicate that success in product, engineering, and customer-facing solutions."

"Thank you for your trust and support," Vision replied. "I couldn't achieve anything without your support and the massive investment in infrastructure. But the timing isn't great. We're in the midst of a huge migration to our new machine learning system, which I'm coordinating. It will take time to get my replacement up to speed."

"Did I mention a replacement?" Expi smiled. "You've always fought against the silos between customer solutions and operations. I'm not replacing you. I'm consolidating all internal and external technology groups under you as the new CTO and eliminating the CIO position."

Vision gasped, pausing to gather her thoughts.

"I've been most impressed by how you collaborate with people and help them grow," Expi continued. "The change in Damon after you started coaching him was nothing short of a miracle. Everyone wanted him out, and now everyone gives him rave reviews. Is it possible for him to step up and take over the coordination efforts so you can focus on customer solutions and products?"

"It sounds very exciting and scary. I'm surprised and flattered. I haven't worked directly with customers. Where are my blind spots?" Vision asked.

"That's a great question for you to explore, Vision," Expi replied. "It's a journey of expansiveness. If you start questioning your old assumptions and redefining yourself in the context of our systems, you will be able to question and redefine everything we do in the context of the systems we exist within."

"That sounds very abstract, Expi. I'm not sure I fully understand what you mean," Vision said.

"It sounds abstract, but it's real. We spend all our time 'in the organization' focusing on 'our goals' to serve 'our customers' to the point that we can't see other organizations, goals, and customers beyond those we've defined. We've narrowed our thinking and ability to create solutions for whatever is in our blind spots."

"I see what you mean," Vision thought aloud. "I'm not thinking or operating that way now, and I don't have the bandwidth to do so even in my current role. How can I manage this in my new position?"

"That's a fantastic question. Making the invisible visible is still a work in progress for me, so I hired an executive coach who specializes in expanding Potential to help evolve our capacity to redefine how we see the world. I believe they will help you make the uncomfortable ambiguity and complexity of your new position comfortable."

"I'm all in," Vision smiled. "Thank you."

My Vision-Centric to Expansive-Transformer Recollection

Three years after integrating Potential development into my practice, I felt confident that I had completed my transformation into the Integral Potential. But I was wrong. My sentence completion Potential assessment revealed that my center of gravity was still Vision-Centric, with growth into the Expansive and fallback into Domain-Centric. Are you kidding me?

Susanne Cook-Greuter, a renowned adult and ego development psychologist, author, and teacher, debriefed my assessment in a conversation that changed my life. Noticing my disappointment at being 'stuck' at Vision-Centric, Susanne surprised me by spending considerable time appreciating and praising the Vision-Centric Potential.

Then I had my aha moment. Susanne helped me realize that setting a goal to elevate my Potential to Integral was, ironically, a major obstacle holding me back. I had made this mistake with myself, and I had made the same mistake with my clients—some of whom were CEOs and senior executives impacting thousands of lives. We were all 'stuck' because we had turned Potential into our goal.

"If it isn't a goal to boost my Potential, what is it?" I asked Susanne.

"It's an outcome," she simply replied.

That response was enough for me to see that in the polarity of Outcome AND Process, I had been prioritizing the outcome over the process. My 40-year career has conditioned me to focus on results. But the more I reflected on this, the more I began to see the process itself as an outcome. A year later, the process and outcome dissolved into one.

This realization was profound. It underscored the importance of embracing the journey, not just the destination. It taught me to value the process as much as the outcome, leading to a more integrated and expansive approach to personal and professional growth.

Vision-Centric Weaknesses

Vision-Centric leaders excel at creating purposeful visions, setting audacious goals, and driving shared outcomes. However, these strengths can also limit their broader perspective in several key ways:

Overemphasis on Outcomes: Vision-Centric leaders are deeply committed to performance indicators, objectives, and key results. This intense focus can lead them to believe they can control all outcomes, overlooking the reality that many factors lie beyond their control.

Neglecting Processes and Relationships: In their pursuit of results, Vision-Centric leaders overlook processes and relationships that don't directly impact outcomes. This can lead to significant sacrifices, neglected relationships, and frustration with work-life balance.

Prioritizing External Over Internal Rewards: While Vision-Centric leaders focus on growth and self-actualization, they often prioritize external rewards over internal fulfillment. They may lack a systemic view of their impact beyond their organizations and have not yet expanded their purpose to include the broader world, society, and communities in which they operate.

Limited Systemic Perspective: Although Vision-Centric leaders can acknowledge various perspectives within their context, they struggle to step outside and observe from a broader systemic viewpoint. This limits their ability to fully understand and address complex issues.

Short-Term Focus: Many Vision-Centric leaders find themselves over-extended and constantly battling time constraints. Their heavy focus on short-term delivery and day-to-day operations often comes at the expense of long-term strategic thinking.

Blind Spots and Defensiveness: These leaders may lack awareness of their blind spots due to insufficient time for reflection. They can become defensive when receiving feedback about their strategies, spending more time advocating than inquiring and listening.

Controlling Tendencies: Vision-Centric leaders often exhibit controlling behaviors, with their identity and self-worth tied to outcomes. This can lead them to stick to well-tested paths, take fewer risks, and overlook flaws in their interactions with stakeholders.

Overworking 'In the Business': They tend to focus heavily on working 'in the business' and less 'on the business,' and similarly, they work 'in their team' and less 'on the team.'

Self-Blame for Failures: Vision-Centric leaders often take on too much responsibility, blaming themselves for failing to achieve goals without fully acknowledging how external factors influence success.

Expansive Transformer Strengths

Breaking Conventional Norms: Leaders at the Expansive Transformer Potential break away from conventional norms and cultural scripts. They transcend traditional behaviors, recognizing the limitations and unexamined assumptions that shaped their previous Potential.

Challenging Beliefs: Expansive Transformers not only explore what they believe but also scrutinize how those beliefs were formed. They understand that beliefs are relative to cultural context, personal experiences, and life circumstances. This insight fosters cultural independence, creativity, and innovation.

Cultivating Agility: Expansive Transformer leaders inspire those around them to experiment and be playful, cultivating a culture of agility within their organizations. They encourage a mindset of flexibility and adaptability.

Systems Thinking: These leaders excel in viewing variables as both whole systems and parts of a larger whole system. This broader perspective enables them to offer insights and solutions that others overlook.

Thinking Beyond Boundaries: Freed from the Vision-Centric focus on outcomes, Expansive leaders think beyond conventional limits. They prioritize people's development as an end in itself rather than merely a means to achieve greater outcomes.

Embracing Risk and Innovation: Expansive leaders are more open to taking risks, making significant reorganizations, eliminating routines, and experimenting with new ways of working. This approach is highly effective in navigating complex situations, allowing them to manage unpredictability without the need for immediate, predictable outcomes.

Empathy and Tolerance: Expansive leaders also demonstrate greater empathy and tolerance for differences, creating a more inclusive and supportive environment.

If these strengths resonate with you, the following sections will guide you in adopting the new Expansive behaviors that will help you acquire these qualities.

Decide on the One Big Shift

While the transition to the Expansive Transformer Potential primarily involves shifts in mindsets, beliefs, and assumptions, there are specific, observable behaviors you can adopt to embody this transformation in action.

Observing and Noticing: Expansive leaders shift their focus from themselves to others, observing and sharing their observations. They pay close attention to how organizational culture influences individual and team behaviors in ways that may limit creativity.

Pausing and Inquiring: Expansive leaders pause during conversations to observe what's happening within themselves and others. They then inquire about it, often using 'time-outs' to ask, "How are we doing?" both individually and as a team. This practice disrupts old patterns, fostering curiosity and encouraging change over mere stability.

Inviting Opposing Points of View: While most leaders naturally prefer buy-in over resistance, Expansive leaders actively invite challenges and appreciate different points of view, which is essential for fostering innovation.

Questioning Everything: Expansive leaders continually question their own and their organization's purpose, vision, values, strategies, and processes to ensure alignment and openness to change.

Challenging the Norms: Expansive Transformers challenge existing business practices and collaboration methods. They move away from a rational, stable culture toward one that is creative, innovative, collaborative, and transformational.

Listening Deeply: Expansive leaders practice deep listening—not just to acknowledge and repeat but to understand the meaning behind what is being said. This approach fosters deeper understanding and connection.

By choosing any one of these behaviors as your One Big Shift, you can begin your transition from Vision-Centric to Expansive Transformer Potential.

Identify Counter Behaviors

The behaviors that hinder transformation into the Expansive Potential are often overextensions of Vision-Centric 'positive' traits. When these behaviors are pushed too far, they can lead to negative side effects and diminish their intended benefits. Here are some examples:

Controlling the Agenda: Vision-Centric leaders have a clear North Star but may struggle to consider other competing visions or perspectives.

Ignoring Soft Issues: Their focus on measurable results can lead to neglecting important but less quantifiable aspects of the organization.

Dominating Meetings: Vision-Centric leaders often take up more airtime to push their vision, leaving little room for others to challenge or contribute.

Driving Excessively Hard: An obsession with results can blind them to the personal and long-term consequences for themselves and others, risking burnout and compromising sustainability.

Defending Against Intrusions: Over-defending their vision can lead to dismissing perspectives and feedback that might be valuable for strategic growth.

Solving Unsolvable Problems: They may try to choose between options when both are necessary, leading to ineffective decision-making.

Overwhelmed by Ideas: Getting caught up in too many ideas and goals can create chaos. For example, a CEO I worked with frequently changed direction towards 'new shiny objects,' creating frustration among the team.

Neglecting Details: A focus on the big picture can result in overlooking essential details. Visionaries need 'linears' to execute, while 'linears' need visionaries to innovate.

Neglecting Personal Needs and Relationships: Ignoring personal well-being and important relationships can lead to imbalance and dissatisfaction.

Compartmentalizing Issues: Failing to connect interdependencies can create inefficiencies and missed opportunities.

Not Evaluating Assumptions: Overlooking the subjectivity behind perceived objectivity can lead to flawed decision-making.

Working Too Hard for Buy-In: Focusing excessively on securing agreement rather than engaging in genuine inquiry can stifle diverse input and collaboration.

Directing Everything: Attempting to control all outcomes can result in autocratic behavior contrary to the leader's intentions.

These counterproductive behaviors are often driven by two overextended positive attributes:

Over-Ambition: When leaders' identities and self-worth are tied to outcomes, they may push too hard to get ahead, seek credit excessively, and compete with others, sometimes to the detriment of collaboration.

Over-Drive: An excessive drive can become compulsive, making it difficult to relax and let go. Leaders may take on unrealistically high workloads and set a precedent that others must work similarly long hours.

These counterproductive behaviors are frequently rooted in underlying fears, which we will explore next.

Connect to Fears that Drive Counter Behaviors

Vision-Centric leaders are often motivated by a deep fear of failing to achieve their goals. For many CEOs, the greatest concern is falling short of growth targets. Another major source of anxiety is the lack of control and the feeling of helplessness when they cannot dictate outcomes or take ownership of results.

When Vision-Centric leaders attempt to engage in Expansive behaviors, they often express these fears during coaching sessions:

- Being dependent
- Losing control
- Being just one among many
- Not meeting their standards or goals
- Being cast in stereotypes
- Not accomplishing
- Not learning
- Failing to execute
- Missing deadlines and milestones
- Being incompetent
- Missing opportunities
- Slowing down
- Being interrupted/disrupted
- Being overwhelmed

Compared to the fears of earlier Potentials, which often revolve around how they are perceived ('seen'), Vision-Centric fears focus more on their state of 'being.' This distinction emphasizes that Vision-Centric is the only **independent** Potential, while the three preceding Potentials are **dependent,** and the three succeeding Potentials are **interdependent**.

Reflect on your own fears. Do you have fears not mentioned above? Can you connect with these fears and see how they influence your counterproductive behaviors? Understanding these fears is the first step toward overcoming the obstacles to your transformation.

Construct Restraining Assumptions

By now, you know the drill. Connect the 'if' behaviors with 'then' fears to reveal the deeply ingrained assumptions within your operating system. Here's what this looks like in practice:

- If I ask too many questions, I'll be disrupted
- If I listen too much to others, I won't accomplish anything
- If I try to integrate other perspectives, I'll lose control
- If I don't get buy-in, I won't execute
- If I try to connect the dots, I'll lose precious time and miss opportunities and deadlines
- If I'm hands-off, I'll become dependent on others
- If I don't solve the problems, I'm incompetent

What behaviors trigger your fears? Have you recognized the automatic assumptions your mind makes without your consent?

Release Confining Safeguards

Whether we're aware or unaware of our fears, our subconscious mind creates safeguards to protect us from the 'big bad' assumptions. Like previous Potentials, these safeguards are identity, self-worth, footholds, equals, and rules.

Vision-Centric Identity

In scholarly circles, the Vision-Centric identity is often described as Self-Authoring (a term coined by Harvard Professor Robert Kegan) . This identity is characterized by independence and a strong sense of personal agency. It revolves around the ability to predict outcomes and achieve set goals. Here are the typical identities of a Vision-Centric leader:

- I'm the master of my destiny
- I'm my success
- I'm results-oriented (I'm my results)
- I'm whatever I aspire to be
- I'm a high achiever
- I'm a high performer
- I'm decisive
- I'm effective
- I'm independent

In a capitalist context, these identities are not only rewarded but also admired. This is why expanding beyond these identities often triggers fear and is seen as a threat to our success. As a result, these identities act as both a safeguard and a constraint, protecting us while also limiting our growth beyond the Vision-Centric Potential.

Consider the following questions to delve deeper into your Vision-Centric identity:

- Which of these identities resonate with you?
- Are there any additional identities that shape your self-view?
- Reflect on moments when you describe yourself. What "I am..." statements do you often use?

Understanding these aspects can reveal how your Vision-Centric identity might be holding you back from evolving into more expansive Potentials.

Vision-Centric Self-worth

For leaders rooted in the Vision-Centric Potential, self-worth is intricately tied to their professional achievements and the acceptance of their strategic vision.

- My self-worth is linked to how well my vision is embraced by my board, peers, and team.
- I feel worthy when my strategies are supported across all levels.
- My sense of worth diminishes if I fail to deliver the expected results.
- I question my worth when I am indecisive.

Vision-Centric leaders often experience guilt over poor decisions and regret over missed opportunities, which can heighten feelings of being an impostor or doubts about their capabilities. This heightened sense of responsibility for outcomes can lead to imposter syndrome, where, despite external successes, they internally feel fraudulent or inadequate.

The link between identity and self-worth is closely intertwined—threats to one can destabilize the other. As we transition toward Transformer Potentials, the reliance on identity and self-worth as safeguards diminishes. This shift happens because these concepts are deeply ego-driven. Moving into Transformer Potentials involves gradually letting go of the ego, allowing for a broader and more inclusive understanding of self-worth. Instead of focusing on individual achievements, this new perspective emphasizes collective progress and transformation.

Vision-Centric Footholds

Vision-Centric leaders often embrace the mantra famously attributed to Peter Drucker: "If you can't measure it, you can't manage it." While they focus on measurable outcomes, they may overlook intangible results and costs.

Here are common footholds Vision-Centric leaders may struggle to let go of:

Linear Logic: They cling to step-by-step planning and linear cause-and-effect reasoning, even though progress is often non-linear or exponential.

Analytical Thinking: Reliance on logical conclusions drawn from data and experience creates a perceived objectivity while ignoring inherent biases and assumptions that shape our 'reality.'

Juggling Many Balls: They experience high tension between opposing or competing strategies, viewing them as separate and unrelated issues.

Agreeing to Disagree: This approach is used in an attempt to achieve alignment where none exists, often avoiding necessary confrontations or discussions.

Personal Views Aside: They may push aside personal perspectives to advance an agenda, not realizing this can create barriers that erode intimacy and understanding.

Focus on the Positives: By concentrating only on positive aspects, they shield their vision from doubt and criticism, controlling emotions to achieve goals.

Never-Ending Commitment: A perpetual sense of urgency leads to an unrealistic workload, leaving no time for reflection or living in the present. Phrases like "I'm totally squeezed right now" or "I wish I had time to reflect" are common.

Making it All Happen: They often feel an unrealistic sense of ownership and responsibility for achieving goals, lacking clear boundaries.

Living in the Future: A focus on future outcomes can prevent them from staying present in the moment.

Fully Independent: This mindset overlooks the necessary interdependence within larger, overarching systems.

Changing the World: Vision-Centric leaders might fail to recognize how the world is also changing them.

Mobilizing Resources: In their focus on mobilization, they may miss emergent opportunities in the present.

Finding the Root Cause: In crises, the quest to understand how things "are" can lead to over-analysis, as I experienced during a company crisis in India when immediate action was needed, yet I was caught up in finding a root cause.

Self-Determination: They may have a deep conviction that their strategy is superior, rationalizing decisions based on clear criteria without pausing to consider probable missteps or alternative viewpoints.

Predicting the Future: They possess strong certainty about future outcomes, relying heavily on data to shape what comes next. However, this reliance often occurs without critically examining the assumptions underpinning the forecasts.

I held onto these footholds for years. Which of these footholds are you still holding onto?

Vision-Centric Equals

Vision-Centric leaders often equate success solely with results, performance, and outcomes. I recall coaching a CEO who was devastated because his attempt to sell his company, after ten years of effort, had failed. He measured his entire success by this sale and viewed himself as a failed entrepreneur. In doing so, he overlooked the immense value of the company he had nurtured, the connected and caring team he had built, and the effective organization they had created together.

Here are common equals of Vision-Centric leaders:

- Success = Results
- Prediction = Future
- Solving problems = Generating solutions
- Optimization = Effectiveness
- Choices = Independence
- Prioritization = Decisions-making
- Advocating = Change others' minds
- Complexity = Contradictions = Inconsistencies
- Feedback = Growth
- Mistakes = Learning opportunities

Some of these equations are deeply embedded in the systems within which executives operate. For instance, CEOs presenting budgets to their boards are expected to predict the future with certainty, almost like fortune tellers. In such a context, acknowledging uncertainty is often viewed unfavorably.

What are your own equations? How do they serve as safeguards for you? And how do they hold you back?

Vision-Centric Rules

Expansive Transformer is the last Potential to be governed by explicit rules, though it involves fewer than earlier Potentials. Over time, many of these rules have become clichés:

- **Think outside the box**: Encouraging innovative thinking
- **It's all about the results**: Focusing primarily on outcomes

- **Change is the only constant**: Emphasizing adaptability
- **Backed by science, frameworks, and models**: Valuing evidence-based approaches
- **We need to be rational**: Prioritizing logical over emotional decisions
- **Getting things done**: Highlighting efficiency and task completion
- **Matter of fact**: Valuing direct and clear communication

Creativity and leadership are foundational for Vision-Centric leaders, embodying the essence of steering one's own course. Reflect on the rules you adhere to: How do they protect your approach, and in what ways might they limit your Potential?

Pair Beliefs with Interdependent Beliefs

Transformer Potentials excel in identifying and effectively leveraging polarities, embracing both poles rather than favoring one. In contrast, Vision-Centric leaders typically favor the left pole in the following common polarities:

- Goal AND Experience
- Outcome AND Process
- Change the World AND Change Myself
- Predicting AND Sensing
- Controlling AND Letting Go
- Open to Feedback AND Accept Feedback
- Doing AND Being
- Future AND Present
- Science AND Art
- Analytical AND Intuitive
- Achieving AND Questioning

Centric leaders often gravitate towards the left poles of various polarities, but transitioning to the Expansive Potential requires embracing also the right poles.

One of the most profound challenges is understanding the polarity between 'Doing' and 'Being.' Many have struggled to differentiate between these concepts. Essentially, 'doing' is represented by verbs—actions we take—while 'being' is described by adjectives—states or qualities we embody. This distinction is crucial, not just a lesson in grammar.

In my practice, I often work with clients who are predominantly action-oriented, particularly those at the Vision-Centric or earlier Potentials. They tend to describe their activities in terms of verbs.

Here's an exercise to help you explore this: write down three verbs that describe your actions ('doing') and three adjectives that describe your state of being. Can you see the connection between them? For example, "listening" (doing) happens when I am "present" (being), and "asking tough questions" (doing) occurs when I am feeling "courageous" or "curious" (being).

During my journey towards the Expansive Potential, I focused on three states of 'being':

- **Observer**: I reflect on the objectivity of my observations, recognizing how my conditioning influences my thoughts. I strive to see separate variables as parts of a larger whole and part of another whole.
- **Questioner**: I continually challenge my beliefs, uncover hidden social and cultural assumptions, and work to make these visible to both myself and others.
- **Relativist**: I consider my beliefs within the context of my cultural up-bringing, personal experiences, and life circumstances, acknowledging that sometimes there is no clear way to prioritize among competing perspectives.

Now it's your turn. Reflect on the polarities in your life. Which right poles have you been neglecting? How can you balance 'doing' with 'being' to effectively leverage both sides of these polarities?

Transforming from Vision-Centric to Expansive Transformer
Reflection Practice

Crossing the threshold from Centric to Transformer Potentials starts with consistent reflection. It's important to dedicate a few minutes each day to pause and consider the changes you're striving for in your behaviors and current state of being. Reflection involves examining your actions, feelings, and thoughts in depth:

- **Doing**: What changes are needed in my actions and behaviors?
- **Feeling**: What emotions are linked to these actions? What feelings arise in specific situations?
- **Thinking**: What's happening in my mind? What is my internal dialogue? Are my thoughts subjective or objective? In what ways might I be mistaken?

Here are some guiding questions to help deepen your self-reflection:

- If I were financially free, what would I choose to do for the rest of my life?
- What kind of culture do I want to create?
- What societal issues upset me the most?
- What do I notice in my body when my feelings fluctuate in different situations?
- What are my core values?
- What virtues do I wish to develop?
- To whom am I truly loyal, and what does loyalty mean to me?
- What do I find most beautiful?
- What would I be like if I were more empathic and patient with people?
- How would I be different if I were free from my fears?

Leverage Both Outcomes and Processes

My transformation was notably slow because I initially focused too heavily on outcomes rather than processes. For instance, during calls with prospective customers, my primary goal was to secure the business. This focus led me to control the conversation and push my agenda rather than engaging naturally with the flow of the dialogue.

Everything changed when I shifted my attention from merely achieving outcomes to genuinely engaging in the process of the conversation itself. At first, this felt paradoxical—how could focusing less on outcomes lead to better results? Yet, polarities in our goals and actions can often appear paradoxical until we fully engage with them.

The real insight came when I began to value both the process and the outcome equally, allowing them to merge seamlessly. This integration eased the tension between them. Over time, the process itself became my outcome. Even if a business deal did not succeed, I found fulfillment in the meaningful connections and value created during the interactions. This perspective reshaped my approach, turning each conversation into a fulfilling experience, regardless of the immediate commercial results.

Systemic Awareness

Jacob, the Chief Revenue Officer at a tech company, was highly respected for his leadership and renowned for orchestrating global sales summits that were nothing short of masterpieces. His ability to create memorable experiences motivated his team long-term. His direct reports, top-tier performers who could easily held Jacob's position elsewhere, chose to stay because of the enriching culture he fostered. Despite frequent changes in the compensation plan, attrition remained remarkably low—a testament to his effective leadership.

However, Jacob's first 360-degree assessment uncovered a surprising gap in his systemic awareness. He realized he had been viewing the sales division as his entire universe, neglecting the broader organizational context. Although he was responsible for revenue growth, he had not fully engaged with the company's overall profitability or its external systems and sustainability efforts.

This realization prompted a significant shift in his leadership approach. He began to view the senior leadership team as his "first team" rather than solely focusing on his global sales team.

By recognizing the senior leadership team as his "first team," Jacob embraced a broader perspective. He started making decisions with the entire organization in mind, not just sales. This holistic approach not only enhanced his leadership effectiveness but also aligned his actions with those of the CEO, contributing to the overall well-being of the company.

A key shift for Jacob was understanding that, unlike the CEO who oversees the entire organization, other executives, including himself, had been managing their specific functions—finance (CFO), marketing (CMO), operations (COO), etc. If asked about their team, they would typically refer to the team they lead rather than the team they belong to.

Leaders who transition into the Expansive Potential outgrow their specific functions, adopting a CEO-like perspective that encompasses the entire organization and beyond.

Practice Inquiry

In conversations, Vision-Centric leaders often spend most of their time advocating their own point of view and the least time exploring others' perspectives. They focus on securing "buy-in" but rarely ask meaningful questions.

Expansive Transformers, on the other hand, inquire as much as they advocate. While this might sound simple—just ask more questions—the true essence of inquiry involves genuine curiosity about other perspectives and a clear sense of purpose.

It's more than just asking questions for the sake of it. Many people try asking questions but do not sustain this behavior for long. True inquiry is about having a real curiosity about other viewpoints and understanding what the inquiry is in service of.

The key is to transform statements into questions and turn observations into hypotheses. This approach not only gathers information but also deepens understanding and facilitates meaningful dialogue. For instance, instead of stating, "We need to improve our client engagement," ask, "How might we better understand our clients' needs?" This shift from a declarative to an inquisitive stance encourages more collaborative and thoughtful responses, leading to a deeper exploration of issues.

This method is central to being an Expansive Transformer: constantly seeking to understand and reframe the discourse, which enriches the decision-making process.

Build Trust with Deep Listening

Expansive Transformers excel in building trust through deep listening, utilizing two distinct channels: analytical and empathic.

Analytical Channel: This channel focuses on examining strategic and technical challenges, identifying alignments and misalignments, and asking probing questions to enhance understanding of rational data. It's a familiar approach in professional settings, where the goal is often to solve problems or gather more information.

Empathic Channel: This channel shifts the focus from 'me' to 'them,' fostering intimacy and building trust by engaging with non-rational data. It involves genuinely stepping into another person's experience to understand their emotional state and the stakes involved for them.

Deep listening integrates three crucial components:

1. **What do they feel?**
   Identifying and naming other people emotions can help engage them more effectively. To do this, it's important to expand your own emotional vocabulary so you can express their feelings.

2. **What's important for them?**
   Understanding what the other person stands to gain or lose—whether it's integrity, credibility, or respect—illuminates why the conversation matters to them. What's at stake for them?

3. **How do they make sense?**
   Instead of just asking, "What's going on?" try hypothesizing about their experience and then verifying it. Meaning making is the process of trying to understand and express how people make sense of what's happening. This sense-making helps you connect more deeply with them.

Deep listening is a humble guess about the person's **feelings, needs, and experiences.**

Here are a few examples:

- "So, it feels unsafe to take that initiative?"
- "Is it like you're feeling boxed in?"
- "Does this situation feel too risky for you?"
- "Are you feeling unsettled because people aren't relying on you?"
- "Did you feel relieved when the board supported your decision?"

- "Do you feel like you're losing control when you push the 'Send' button?"
- "Are you (feeling)...?"
- "Is it about...?"
- "Are you worried about that...?"
- "Is it almost like...?"

These inquiries are designed not to assert correctness but to genuinely explore another person's perspective with curiosity and empathy. By framing our questions as check-ins, we invite correction and foster understanding, presenting our assumptions as possibilities for discussion rather than certainties. This method of deep listening involves making educated guesses about someone's feelings, needs, and experiences, and then validating these hypotheses through empathetic engagement. It's not about having the right answer but about grasping the other's perceived reality, which can profoundly enhance relationships, especially with loved ones, turning every interaction into an opportunity for deeper connection and trust.

Test Assumptions

Testing our assumptions involves trying to disprove them. This is done by engaging in behaviors related to these assumptions and observing the outcomes in controlled, low-risk situations. This approach allows us to assess the validity of assumptions our subconscious may have accepted as true, even if they are false.

We start with simpler scenarios to ensure we have the mental space to notice how others react and to reflect on our own actions, thoughts, and feelings. High-stakes situations can prevent us from effectively testing our assumptions and might even reinforce them.

For example, I once believed that relinquishing control would lead to unsatisfactory results and frustration. To challenge this, I chose a low-risk scenario: allowing my family to decide on restaurants for our celebrations. We often debated between Italian, Chinese, Indian, or Mediterranean cuisine. As a health-conscious vegan, stepping back from controlling the choice was challenging, but it allowed me to observe the impact on everyone involved. I found that by not imposing my preferences, I reduced tension and made our gatherings more enjoyable. This positive outcome demonstrated that my assumption was flawed and highlighted the broader benefits of letting go, making the experience better for all. This served as a successful, safe, small-scale test of my assumption.

Develop 4-D Thinking

4-D thinking represents an advanced level of cognitive perspective-taking, building upon simpler forms of thinking found at earlier Potential levels. It involves a dynamic, multi-dimensional approach that incorporates various perspectives and broadens decision-making processes. Here's a breakdown of how thinking evolves across different dimensions:

1-D Thinking (First-Person Perspective): This level of thinking is characterized by viewing situations solely from one's own mindset. Individuals at the Self-Centric Potential see the world only through their personal lens, often imposing this perspective on others without considering or acknowledging different viewpoints.

2-D Thinking (Second-Person Perspective): This level of thinking allows individuals to see, relate to, and acknowledge perspectives outside their own. Associated with the Group and Domain-Centric Potentials, this thinking stage involves understanding and appreciating viewpoints from other people, enhancing collaboration and empathy within group settings.

3-D Thinking (Third-Person Perspective): This perspective enables individuals to view situations from all aspects within the system in which they operate, going beyond personal and direct interpersonal considerations. It is a hallmark of the Vision-Centric Potential, characterized by a strength in asking probing questions with deep curiosity. This level of thinking fosters the realization that different perspectives can all hold truth—a concept that 1-D and 2-D thinking often overlook. 3-D thinking is crucial for comprehensive system analysis and integration.

4-D Thinking (Fourth-Person Perspective): This expansive mode of thinking allows individuals to engage in truly multi-dimensional thinking, seamlessly shifting between advocating their own perspectives and inquiring into others'. It is the hallmark of the Expansive Potential, where understanding transcends the immediate and obvious, integrating a broader range of perspectives into decision-making.

Here are a few strategies to develop 4-D thinking:

1. **Identify Your Primary Stakeholders:** In my experience, teams rarely agree quickly on who the primary stakeholders are without some discussion. The key criterion for determining primary stakeholders is their importance to the company's future.
2. **Step into Their Shoes:** Assign one or two team members to represent the primary stakeholders during meetings. Observe the dialogue from both rational and emotional perspectives. This exercise often provides unexpected insights, enriching the conversation significantly.
3. **Develop Systemic Relationships with Stakeholders:** Typically, only one or two executives engage directly with key stakeholders, such as customers or board members. By involving the entire team in these interactions, everyone gains access to systemic thinking from diverse viewpoints. Explore what can be achieved collaboratively that would be impossible alone. Aim for a tripartite win: for you, for the stakeholders, and for the broader ecosystem they influence (stakeholders' stakeholders).
4. **Avoid Selling or Promoting Solutions in Relationship-Building Meetings:** Focus on building relationships rather than pushing agendas. This approach fosters deeper understanding and collaboration.

5. **Always Inquire, Don't Just Advocate:** Make a conscious effort to inquire as much as you advocate. This promotes a culture of curiosity and open dialogue, which is essential for 4-D thinking.

6. **Shift Stakeholder Engagement from Transactional to Relational:** Move your interactions from mere transactions to meaningful partnerships. This shift deepens engagement and aligns objectives more closely with shared success.

7. **Collect Data About Stakeholders' Perspectives:** Use collective assessments to understand stakeholders' views comprehensively. This helps develop a 4-D perspective by considering multiple dimensions of stakeholder relationships.

These strategies are designed to expand your thinking beyond traditional dimensions, enabling a richer, more interconnected approach to leadership and decision-making.

The Bottom Line

The transition from Vision-Centric to Expansive Transformer represents a profound shift—one that only 15% of leaders achieve. This transformation is both challenging and disorienting, as it requires a deep reevaluation of fundamental assumptions, beliefs, and values that have long guided us.

During this transformation, some leaders make radical changes: they might quit their jobs, switch careers, or launch new ventures as they discover new guiding stars. Others stay within their corporate roles, adapting their new mindsets to existing structures while continuing to leverage their Vision-Centric skills in an outcome-driven business world shaped by stock exchanges, private equity, and venture capital firms.

The Expansive Transformer Potential unlocks 4-D perspectives previously inaccessible at the Vision-Centric stage, fostering systemic thinking that can significantly influence outcomes—especially when those outcomes are no longer the primary focus. However, the journey doesn't end here; the Integral Transformer represents the ultimate stage of Potential. Therefore, it's wise not to remain at the Expansive stage for too long but to continue progressing to the next chapter of your developmental journey.

CHAPTER 9.

FROM EXPANSIVE TO INTEGRAL AND UNITIVE TRANSFORMER

In a world marked by growing complexity and uncertainty, many current CEOs would likely not be reappointed by their boards. Instead, boards are turning to Integral Transformers as the next generation of leaders. These Integral leaders excel at navigating complex challenges with ease, fostering engagement with a sense of playfulness, and making decisions that are free from ego.

If you've successfully made the challenging leap from Vision-Centric to Expansive Transformer, you're already halfway to reaching the Integral Potential. The good news is that the progression from Expansive to Integral is generally smoother and more natural. So, if the transition is relatively straightforward, why have only 5% of leaders achieved it?

From my coaching experience, leaders are often stuck at the Expansive Potential or retreat back to the Vision-Centric Potential for three reasons:

1. Premature Transition: Some leaders rush through the transformation without fully integrating the lessons and experiences of earlier Potentials. Without this comprehensive integration, achieving a true Integral state becomes impossible.
2. Identity Discomfort: Others find themselves intimidated by their own transformation, feeling as though their new self is unfamiliar, perhaps even too noble. This discomfort signals an incomplete integration at the Expansive stage.
3. Misunderstanding the Journey: The framing of the Expansive Potential as a 'pit stop' rather than a 'parking lot' may have misled some. The key is to find balance—progressing through the Expansive stage without rushing, but not lingering too long and getting stuck in confusion.

What's the ideal timing? Transitioning in less than six months might be too quick, while taking more than a year could feel overly prolonged. However, this timeline varies greatly, as the process is more art than science, and every leader's journey is unique.

Expi Story

The board meeting had gone better than Expi expected. He had invested extra time in one-on-one discussions with key board members to secure full support for the planned acquisition—a significant and high-stakes endeavor. Acquisitions are unpredictable; no matter how thorough the due diligence is, what you see before the acquisition isn't always what you get afterward.

Expi was looking forward to unwinding at home after a stressful month of navigating the acquisition with investment banks and the board of the acquired company. But his plans shifted unexpectedly when Integra, the board chairperson, requested a private conversation with him.

This request was unusual for Integra, who typically didn't mince words. Without any preliminary small talk, he dropped a bombshell. "Expi, I have been diagnosed with colon cancer and will not be able to serve as chairman for the coming year, and perhaps never again," Integra said with unsettling calmness.

"I'm so sorry to hear that, Integra. This must be a very scary and confusing time for you," Expi responded, his voice laden with empathy.

"It's early stage. I'll probably survive, given the treatment plan, but there's a high risk of recurrence. The real issue I want to discuss is that I'm not ready to quit my position, nor am I fully able to serve during my recovery. After much deliberation with other board members, we've decided that you should serve as Chairperson and CEO for the year I'm away."

"That's a lot to take in," Expi remarked. "You've always believed that CEOs should never also be board chairs because of the conflict of interest. What changed?"

"Nothing has changed my perspective, Expi," Integra assured him. "I still uphold that belief, but I consider you an exception because of your ability to hold and balance opposite perspectives without being attached to any. I believe you can manage it effectively, albeit with some external support."

"Thank you for your trust. I accept the challenge," Expi acknowledged. "What do you mean by external support?"

"Your ability to navigate multiple possibilities is your greatest strength but also your Achilles heel. Sometimes, you seem lost among the various options, struggling to ground yourself in a decisive action that reconciles differences while advancing our goals swiftly. I attribute my successful transition from founder to chairperson largely to my executive coach, whose name, believe it or not, is Unity. Would you like me to arrange a discovery call with them?"

"Yes, I would," Expi agreed, adding, "I pray for your swift recovery and return to normal life and to reclaim your position as chairperson."

Expansive Transformer Weaknesses

Expansive Transformers, known for challenging assumptions and questioning the so-called 'scientific' certainty of reality, often leave others puzzled with remarks like, "I never know where they're coming from." Those at earlier Potential levels struggle with the concept of relativism, making it difficult for them to relate to leaders who embrace their uniqueness and live fully in the moment.

These leaders are sometimes seen as inconsistent because of their tendency to frequently reinvent processes, introduce innovative ideas, and shift paradigms. Expansive leaders challenge the status quo, rigorously examining not only their company's processes and values but also their own judgments and decisions.

This intense scrutiny can sometimes result in self-doubt and organizational confusion, overshadowing their innovative contributions. As a result, others may focus more on their non-conformity than on their creativity.

A major challenge for Expansive leaders is navigating between two worlds: the rational, traditional, and culture-preserving world of the Vision-Centric and the creative, collaborative, transformational world of the Integral Transformer. In this space, Expansive leaders often question their place within the organization and society, occasionally feeling marginalized in their own environments.

While their inclusiveness encourages broad exploration and consensus-building, it can also lead to decision-making paralysis. Their strong commitment to equality may sometimes hinder their ability to make tough calls in moments of disagreement.

Ultimately, the journey to becoming an Integral Transformer requires a delicate balance—integrating the pragmatic strengths of the Vision-Centric perspective with the deep, insightful approaches of the Expansive Transformer.

Integral Transformer Strengths

Integral Transformers excel in understanding various perspectives and recognizing the interdependencies within complex systems. This deep insight enables them to be exceptionally inclusive and people-oriented leaders.

A key trait of Integral Transformers is their profound empathy for colleagues at earlier Potentials. By reflecting on their own journey through these stages, they understand others' limitations and tailor their communication to connect effectively with diverse individuals and audiences.

Integral Transformers strike a balance between focusing on processes and achieving results. This dual approach helps them identify biases and patterns that others might miss, enhancing their understanding of how different systems interact and influence one another. They are known for changing both the rules of the game and the game itself.

Unlike their predecessors, who often reflect on their actions and decisions after the fact, Integral Transformers practice real-time reflection during activities. This ability to think and adapt on the fly allows them to influence meetings and decisions dynamically, making immediate course corrections when needed.

Integral leaders see no boundaries with external systems and excel at spotting patterns and opportunities across companies, industries, markets, and countries. This broad perspective enables them to devise and communicate complex solutions in simple, understandable ways, leveraging big-picture thinking and long-term planning.

Ultimately, Integral Transformers serve as catalysts for transformative change, impacting multiple areas, including personal, relational, organizational, and economic spheres.

Decide on the One Big Shift

The transition from an Expansive to an Integral Transformer is almost seamless. Integral behaviors deepen the exploration of contextual issues, shifting the focus from the individual to the collective.

Influence and Being Influenced: Unlike earlier Potentials that focus primarily on influencing others, Integral Transformers engage in a reciprocal dynamic where they both influence and are influenced. This mutual exchange allows them to shape and be shaped by their environment.

Collaborate Across: Integral Transformers thrive in collaborative environments. They often approach meetings with flexible agendas, preferring to co-create these agendas dynamically with participants. This fosters a genuine sense of collective ownership and interdependence.

Reframe Context: Attuned and present, Integral Transformers listen intently, using real-time insights to reframe discussions. This ability to reinterpret the content, context, and subtext of conversations enriches dialogue and deepens understanding among all participants.

Co-create Vision: By involving others in the vision-creation process, Integral Transformers ensure that the vision is not only shared but deeply committed to by all contributors, enhancing alignment and motivation across teams.

Innovate Systemically: Their innovation goes beyond financial metrics to address broader developmental, social, and environmental challenges, reflecting a comprehensive approach to entrepreneurship.

Integrate Diverse Perspectives: Integral Transformers excel at navigating conflicting opinions to synthesize decisions that respect and incorporate diverse viewpoints.

Design Solutions for Complexity: They possess a unique ability to design solutions tailored to complex, multi-system contexts while simplifying these solutions for clarity and accessibility.

Make Dynamic Decisions: Integral Transformers make decisions with long-term impacts in mind, prioritizing systemic health and sustainability over short-term gains.

Expose Blind Spots: Integral Transformers make the invisible visible. They meticulously observe and highlight overlooked aspects of situations, tackling them head-on. By actively seeking diverse perspectives, they refine strategies and actions for greater effectiveness.

Encouraging Conflict: Integral Transformers view conflicts as opportunities for growth. They engage in disagreements not for confrontation but to uncover underlying differences in values and perspectives, enriching the organizational culture.

Giving and Receiving Transformational Feedback: Integral Transformers seek and provide feedback that goes beyond incremental adjustments, aiming to foster significant developmental changes. This feedback addresses underlying values, beliefs, emotions, and assumptions.

This holistic approach prepares Integral Transformers to handle the complexities of modern leadership and equips them to drive meaningful change across various domains, setting a new standard for leadership effectiveness.

Identify Counter Behaviors

The Expansive Potential is crucial for transitioning to Integral Transformer behaviors, but it also presents certain challenges. Below are some counterproductive behaviors that may arise as Expansive leaders shed old paradigms and embrace new approaches of interaction and decision-making:

Losing Focus on Outcomes: In moving away from the narrow Vision-Centric obsession with results, some Expansive leaders might overcorrect and diminish their drive to achieving tangible outcomes. While prioritizing personal and collective growth is essential, Expansive leaders must also demonstrate a results-oriented mindset.

Overemphasizing Individualism: As Expansive leaders develop a stronger sense of individualism, they might struggle to maintain alignment with their teams and broader organizational goals. This can create friction and misalignment within teams.

Excessive Questioning: An important nature of the Expansive Potential involves questioning long-held beliefs and assumptions. When this questioning extends from self-reflection to probing others, it can cause discomfort or resistance among those not on the same developmental path. Transforming teams collectively can help members understand the journey together and reduce friction.

Delayed Decision-Making: The Expansive leader's emphasis on egalitarian values and consensus can occasionally slow down decision-making processes. While fostering inclusion is vital, it may hinder prompt resolutions and actions, especially in fast-paced environments.

Over-Initiating Without Follow-Through: Expansive leaders frequently introduce numerous initiatives, which can overwhelm both themselves and their teams, ultimately hindering effective execution.

Such behaviors can marginalize Expansive leaders within their organizations, making them appear aloof or disconnected from reality. Recognizing and addressing these counter behaviors allows leaders to identify the underlined fears that generate them.

Connect to Fears that Drive Counter Behaviors

Like the preceding Potentials, the path to embracing Integral behaviors is marked by fears and anxieties that may impede their growth and effectiveness:

- **Regressing to Earlier Potentials:** There is a significant fear of reverting to the more limiting behaviors of earlier Centric Potentials, losing the advancements made in their transformative journey.
- **Remaining Biased:** Despite striving for equality and inclusion, Expansive Transformers worry that unrecognized biases may still influence their decisions and interactions.
- **Losing Presence:** They worry about missing important moments or insights if they are too absorbed in past or future concerns.
- **Feeling Disoriented:** In a world where truth and standards are seen as relative, there is a fear of losing the ability to assert a firm stance on issues, leading to a sense of disorientation.
- **Overlooking Details:** Anxiety about missing critical elements during their thorough explorations as they strive to understand every aspect of their environments.
- **Being Overwhelmed by Complexity:** The urge to grasp too many inter-connections can undermine their ability to form a coherent perspective.
- **Ignoring Dependencies:** There is a fear of failing to recognize the dependencies of actions and decisions shaped by broader contexts and systems.
- **Imposter Syndrome**: Uncovering personal blind spots can lead to feelings of insecurity.
- **Remaining in a Rigid Environment:** There's a persistent concern that, despite their efforts to evolve and implement change, the surrounding culture or systemic structures may resist transformation.
- **Losing Freedom:** They may fear being unable to act freely according to their newly adopted beliefs and values, especially in environments that do not support these changes.

- **Being Misinformed:** As they expand their circle of trust and sources of information, there is a worry about the accuracy and reliability of the information they receive.
- **Unintentionally Discriminating:** In their commitment to equality, they may worry about inadvertently discriminating by favoring certain perspectives over others in their decision-making process.
- **Addressing Symptoms Rather Than Causes:** There is a common fear of focusing too much on surface-level symptoms rather than uncovering and addressing deeper, underlying issues.

Do these concerns resonate with your experiences? Are there other fears you've encountered on your journey toward embracing Integral behaviors? Identifying these fears will help you construct restraining assumptions.

Construct Restraining Assumptions

Expansive Transformers engage in a continuous process of uncovering and examining their internal assumptions. Here are some typical assumptions they construct:

Speed and Oversight: "If I make fast decisions, I will miss part of the picture." This assumption can lead to hesitation and delays, as they fear overlooking critical information.

Outcome Focus: "If I focus too much on outcomes, I will be stuck at Vision-Centric Potential." This drives the need to balance outcome orientation with attention to process and presence.

Questioning Others: "If I don't question others, I'll be unaware of dependencies." This highlights their emphasis on understanding the interconnectedness of systems and people.

Self-Scrutiny: "If I don't question myself, I'll be biased." They recognize the need for self-inquiry to mitigate unconscious biases and ensure fair decision-making.

Innovation and Adaptation: "If I don't initiate a lot of ideas, I'll be stuck in a rigid system." This motivates them to seek continuous innovation to avoid stagnation.

Informed Decisions: "If I don't ask for a lot of opinions, I will be misinformed." It reflects their commitment to inclusivity and gathering diverse perspectives for better decision-making.

Individualism and Freedom: "If I don't leverage individualism, I'm losing my freedom of choice." This relates to their belief in the importance of personal autonomy within collaborative settings.

These assumptions are not exhaustive. Expansive Transformers are encouraged to continually identify and question their own assumptions as part of their growth process. What assumptions have you encountered on your journey? Are there other assumptions you've identified that need challenging or validation?

Release Confining Safeguards

As we evolve through the Transformer Potentials, the role of the ego diminishes, reducing the constraints that once safeguarded our growth.

Expansive Transformer Identity

Expansive Transformers may overly identity with a singular value, often overlooking other important ones. For example:

- **Equality**: They may elevate a value like equality to an extreme, insisting on giving everyone an equal voice, even when it may not be warranted.
- **Uniqueness**: They often celebrate their distinctiveness, seeing their unique approach as a differentiator, whereas Integral and Unitive Transformers harmonize uniqueness with universality.
- **Truth**: They may become fixated on defending their interpretation of truth, obsessing over the validity of each perspective.

What is the identity that you hold to?

Expansive Transformer Self-worth

Expansive Transformers derive their self-worth from their ability to contextualize and see how different cultural contexts have shaped them. I originally thought about naming this Potential Contextual Transformer. Expansive leaders step out of the system they grew up in and see how this context shaped them. Then, they start to question the cultural context they have never challenged before.

Is that true for you, too? If not, what is your self-worth generator?

Expansive Transformer Footholds

New strengths become weaknesses if over-leveraged:

- **Multiple Truths:** Recognizing multiple truths can lead to confusion and a struggle with objectivity.
- **Relativism**: The belief that "everything is relative" can make decision-making challenging.
- **Egalitarianism**: An excessive commitment to egalitarian principles can lead to indecisiveness by trying to honor all perspectives equally.

Do any of these footholds keep you grounded in the Expansive Potential and prevent further growth? Are there any other footholds you've identified?

Expansive Transformer Equals

Expansive leaders continually challenge their assumptions, resulting in fewer equals compared to earlier Potentials:

- **Better = non-hierarchical:** This leads to operating outside traditional frameworks, sometimes to the detriment of organizational structure.
- **Context = meaning:** An overemphasis on context can sometimes overshadow straightforward, practical solutions.
- **Complexity = progress:** Seeing complexity in everything can complicate straightforward issues.
- **Uniqueness = self-expression = independence:** Overvaluing independence based on self-expression can cause missed opportunities for collaboration.

What equals come to your mind?

Expansive Transformer Rules

Expansive Transformers tend to reject traditional rules, creating their own based on inner insights:

- **The inner game runs the outer game:** They recognize the profound influence of internal states on external circumstances.
- **There is no right answer:** They accept that answers depend greatly on context, which can sometimes lead to confusion.
- **I'm not one thing:** They embrace the multiplicity of their identities, recognizing constant change.
- **What you see isn't what you get:** They understand that appearances can be deceiving.
- **If you think you're in control, you aren't:** They acknowledge the limited control they have, recognizing the influence of both visible and invisible forces.

Expansive Transformers navigate a complex interplay of identity, self-worth, and rules, continually challenging and redefining them to foster growth. What rules are you currently challenging, and how are they influencing your transformation?

Expansive Transformer Beliefs

Expansive Transformers develop a deep appreciation for the human aspects of business interactions, balancing their relentless pursuit of results with a strong emphasis on emotional connections. They begin to see emotions—both their own and others'—as valuable data. This ability transforms their view of people from mere tools for achieving success to the very purpose of their efforts. They come to believe that everyone wants to be seen and heard.

This perspective leads to deeper psychological intimacy in relationships, moving beyond traditional trust based solely on credibility and reliability to include emotional bonds. At this stage, engaging with polarities—balancing each strategy, value, belief, and competence with its opposite—becomes crucial. Expansive Transformers approach life as a dynamic game of identifying and leveraging these dualities.

Their language reflects this shift. They avoid restrictive terms like "but" or "either/or," favoring inclusive phrases such as "even though," "despite," and "nonetheless." These phrases signify their ability to reconcile contradictory ideas through "both/and" and "while" constructs.

These evolving beliefs lead them to appreciate that the whole is greater than the sum of its parts. They understand that every part is a whole in itself and that each whole is part of a larger whole. This comprehension enables them to navigate complex situations marked by multiple interdependencies with greater effectiveness.

However, some polarities still challenge Expansive leaders, as they tend to favor the left pole over the right:

- Relative AND Absolute
- People-oriented AND Action/task-oriented
- Now AND Future
- Inquiring AND Integrating
- Learning AND Transforming
- Negotiable AND Non-Negotiable
- Consensus AND Decisiveness
- Adaptive AND Firm
- Process AND Outcome

As we navigate these polarities, we can easily get confused. For example, the polarity of Outcome AND Process in earlier stages now appear reversed to Process AND Outcome. This isn't merely a reversal but rather a correction of earlier over-corrections. Initially, Expansive leaders may have shifted their focus to process, possibly neglecting outcomes. Now, they approach outcomes differently than they did as Vision-Centrics.

What polarities do you find yourself leaning towards? How can you balance both poles effectively? Have you noticed any previous polarities reemerging, such as Outcome AND Process?

My Transformation from Expansive to Integral

I can't pinpoint the exact moment I transitioned to being an Integral Transformer. There were no clear signals or celebrations—it felt more like a surrender than a victory. Surrender to what? To reality itself. Previously, I was constantly focused on bridging the gap between my vision and reality. Then, one day, I realized there was no gap. It wasn't that circumstances had changed; rather, I had changed. I asked myself, "If this is it, then what?" That acceptance was transformative.

Surprisingly, surrendering to reality didn't slow me down. Instead, I became more effective and productive than ever before.

The next phase of my transformation was even more challenging: saying goodbye to my ego. After 60 years together, detaching from it felt like parting with an old friend. Post-ego, my interactions transformed—I no longer felt the need to impress with clever remarks or showcase my brilliance.

This shift was particularly evident in client meetings, where the ego is often most engaged. Rather than talking about myself during introductions, I focused solely on learning about others. This approach not only deflected attention from me but also engaged clients more deeply. The most challenging moments to keep my ego in check were when others prompted, "Tell us about yourself." Yet, by making introductions one-sided and focusing on others, I never faced complaints; everyone enjoyed attention, and my curiosity about others deepened.

My third major shift as an Integral Transformer was to embrace reductionism zealously. I began to describe complex phenomena in simpler, more fundamental terms, stripping away jargon and making complex systems and relationships more accessible through straightforward language. This drive to simplify led to writing this book, aiming to demystify the complex process of Potential development and present it as a clear, approachable system.

Now, let's explore some other transformative experiences my clients have encountered.

Transforming from Expansive to Integral
5-D Thinking

Leaders who have reached the Integral Potential are capable of viewing issues from the perspectives of even the most remote stakeholders.

Remarkably, only about 5% of leaders have developed this 5-D thinking capacity. In contrast, a staggering 50% remain stuck at the 1-D and 2-D levels, unable to engage in 3-D thinking and beyond.

POTENTIAL	THINKING	PERCENTAGE
Self	1-D	5%
Group	1-D, 2-D	10%
Domain	1-D, 2-D	35%
Vision	1-D, 2D, 3-D	30%
Expansive	1-D, 2-D, 3-D, 4-D	15%
Integral	1-D, 2-D, 3-D, 4-D, 5-D	5%

Figure 9 – Thinking Capacity and Potentials

Here are five approaches to developing 5-D thinking capacity:

1. **Future Backward:** Envision the long-term impact of your actions on future generations, allowing this perspective to guide your decisions on long-term perspectives, such as environmental care, climate change, and sustainability.

2. **Past Forward:** Our personal history plays a crucial role in shaping who we are. Reflecting on pivotal moments from our past can offer profound insights into our development and leadership styles. Take a moment to consider three key experiences that have significantly influenced how you lead today. This "past forward" reflection is essential for advancing rapidly in your developmental journey.

3. **Villain Stakeholder:** In strategic meetings, we often neglect to consider the perspective of our competitors. One of the most enlightening exercises I've facilitated involves team members role-playing as our fiercest competitors. They devise strategies to outmaneuver our company, using insider knowledge to simulate possibly devastating competitive moves we might not have otherwise considered. This

exercise frequently uncovers significant blind spots and probable risks within our strategies.

4. **Invisible Stakeholder:** Identifying stakeholders who are not yet on our radar or whom we might be inadvertently overlooking is crucial. These might include groups deeply invested in environmental concerns or human rights—stakeholders who could have a substantial impact on our organization's future. Recognizing these "invisible" stakeholders can shift and broaden our strategic focus.

5. **Exploring External Systems:** Consider how broader external factors— political, economic, social, technological, legal, and environmental— affect your organization. Understanding these influences is vital for strategic planning and can significantly impact how we navigate our business environment.

Developing 5-D thinking empowers leaders to navigate complex, multifaceted situations more effectively, incorporating diverse perspectives into their decision-making processes.

Real-Time Reflection

Accelerating your transformation from an Expansive to an Integral Transformer requires the ability to act and reflect simultaneously. It's a continuous cycle where action informs reflection, and reflection shapes the next action, perpetuating the process.

Achieving real-time observation involves both engaging in the moment and stepping back to observe, akin to dancing on a club floor while simultaneously watching yourself and others from the balcony. Developing this skill is like a gym workout: you perform sets and reps to build strength, speed, and endurance.

Workout Plan for Real-Time Reflection:

1. **Regular Stops:** Pause every hour or between meetings to check in with yourself.
    *   What behaviors, feelings, and thoughts have you noticed about yourself and others?
    *   What might you have missed?
    *   What important points haven't been raised that should have?
2. **Setting Routines:** Establish these reflective pauses at the end of each hour or meeting, aiming for about 5-7 pauses daily, plus one at the end of the day to reflect on home interactions.
3. **Repetition Frequency:** Initially, these pauses can last about one minute—enough time for quick yet insightful reflections, given the brain's rapid processing capabilities.
4. **Increasing Frequency:** After two weeks, introduce mid-meeting reflections. Continue with the same questions, adding this pause halfway through any significant interaction.
5. **Shortening Intervals:** Over the next few weeks, reduce the intervals to every 15 minutes, with reflections shortened to 30 seconds, moving closer to real-time reflection.
6. **Evaluate Changes:** Reflect on how these insights shape your actions, behaviors, thoughts, and feelings. Notice any shifts in how you present yourself in interactions.

One of my toughest challenges when I began flying fighter jets in the Air Force, was comprehending the constant stream of information from two radio channels. I had to listen, process, and respond quickly to ongoing communications from multiple jets on one radio and ground control on another, all while maintaining a mental moving image of the air combat. This demanded a careful balance of engagement and observation, allowing me to maintain a partial focus on all inputs and develop a cohesive understanding of my surroundings.

This practice of splitting attention not only improved my aerial maneuvers but also offered valuable lessons for leadership. It demonstrates how continuous, nuanced awareness can significantly enhance decision-making and situational awareness in high-stakes conversations.

Body Intelligence

Early in their development, leaders primarily rely on intellectual intelligence (IQ). As they evolve to the Vision-Centric stage, they begin to integrate emotional intelligence (EQ), which enhances their ability to understand and manage emotions. However, Expansive Transformers advance further by incorporating body intelligence (BQ), which involves a profound awareness of physical responses and sensations.

Body intelligence is about tuning into how our bodies react in various situations. For instance, it involves recognizing stress or tension—such as clenching our jaws during high-stakes moments or feeling tightness in our chest during difficult discussions. These physical responses often go unnoticed until someone points them out, as I've done with my clients. This awareness can reveal signals previously ignored, like a gut feeling when someone isn't being truthful or physical discomfort when an 'elephant in the room' remains unaddressed.

To enhance body intelligence, Integral leaders I've coached have engaged in various somatic practices. Meditation is a common tool; even a brief daily session of 10 minutes can significantly boost sensitivity to the body's cues. Simple practices, such as monitoring your breathing patterns, conducting body scans, or engaging in guided meditation, can enhance your body intelligence (BQ). Other beneficial practices include yoga, tai chi, dance, and martial arts—all of which help cultivate a deeper understanding of one's physical responses and well-being.

Transformation Story

Packard's promotion to president of the Americas division at a leading global tech company marked a significant leap in responsibility. His new revenue targets were nearly 20 times higher than those in his previous position, with the pressure intensified by the fact that his division was the main driver of the company's revenue growth.

When I began coaching Packard, he was already operating at the Expansive Transformer Potential. His daily reflection practices and proficiency in 4-D thinking enabled him to effectively observe and inquire into dynamics within himself, his team, and his organization.

However, the challenge escalated with the corporate mandate of a 35% growth goal for his division. This surge in expectations elevated stress levels and highlighted the need for augmented Potential. 5-D thinking expanded Packard's perspective to include not only his own systems but also the broader corporate and customer systems.

With this broader perspective, Packard recognized that the challenges they faced were interconnected across various divisions and that solutions couldn't be confined to his own area. This realization prompted him to explore interdependent strategies that could simultaneously integrate multiple solutions.

In the following weeks, Packard worked closely with corporate leadership to initiate a comprehensive restructuring of the company. Concurrently, his team engaged with customers to build new partnerships and explore innovative business models.

As an Integral Transformer, Packard's influence extended beyond his personal and team development. He drove transformative changes that reshaped his division and impacted broader corporate strategies and customer interactions, demonstrating the profound effect of leadership at the Integral Potential.

The Bottom Line

Integral Transformers move beyond the confusion and uncertainty often seen at the Expansive Potential, where identity, assumptions, and long-held beliefs are intensely questioned. These leaders effectively combine the Vision-Centric focus on achieving results with the Expansive Transformer's traits of mindfulness, broadened perspectives, and ecosystemic thinking.

This unique blend allows Integral Transformers to lead effectively large organizations in highly complex environments. They critically assess their own beliefs, recognizing their limitations and understanding that every system exists within a larger system, which is, in turn, part of an even greater one. They are comfortable navigating contradictions and paradoxes, actively seeking out interdependencies and interconnections that enhance their leadership approach.

Looking forward, the ability to operate as an Integral Transformer will become increasingly vital. CEOs and C-suite executives who lack this capacity will struggle to maintain their roles in the evolving corporate landscape.

Is there a need to advance beyond the Integral to the Unitive Transformer Potential? While not necessary, transitioning to a Unitive Transformer represents an elite path that few leaders have taken. Perhaps you will join this exclusive group, pushing the boundaries of leadership and organizational impact even further.

From Integral to Unitive Transformer

The journey from Integral to Unitive Transformer Potential is a path taken by only a rare few—about 0.1% of leaders reach this stage. I must confess,

I am not among them, nor have I coached anyone who has attained this level of development. However, I believe some may have guided me in this direction.

A Unitive Transformer operates not merely as a leader but as a beacon of unity and spiritual depth. This transformation is driven not by necessity but by a profound spiritual quest—an exploration of unity and oneness. As I read about these remarkable individuals, I feel a sense of lightness and expansiveness that sparks my imagination, inspiring me to envision a life fully woven into the rich tapestry of existence.

Unitive Transformers lead with love and wisdom, embodying a unique blend of toughness and kindness, rigor and compassion. They are resolute in their convictions, fully aware of possible consequences but unaffected by them. Free from ego, their actions are solely for the benefit of others, unlinked to titles or accolades. They remain undefended, open to observing, absorbing, and appreciating the world in its entirety.

Regularly engaged in meditation or similar spiritual practices, Unitive Transformers confront and embrace both their darker aspects and their mortality. They see life as a brief moment within the vast expanse of universal time, which informs their profound connection to all things. Their leadership is characterized by love and wisdom, making them not just leaders but also true guides.

Qualities of Unitive Transformers

Unitive Transformers exhibit a profound interplay between their thoughts, feelings, and actions, staying acutely present and attentive to the nuances of each moment. Here are some defining qualities of Unitive Transformers:

Playing with Contrasts: They navigate life's polarities—chaos AND order, joy AND sorrow, life AND death—with a sense of playfulness and humor, viewing these contrasts as interconnected aspects of existence.

Playing with Constructs: Unitive Transformers are adept at choosing their perceptual filters, constructing and deconstructing their realities, and continually questioning their own constructs. They develop meta-models that strive to approximate reality.

Mastering Meaning-Making: They incessantly question how they make sense of their experiences and then question the validity of those questions, perpetually deepening their understanding.

Mentalizing and Emotionalizing: By integrating their emotional responses with cognitive processes, they adapt and evolve their behaviors to fit new understandings and contexts.

Reframing Perspectives: They continuously redefine and reinterpret their perceptions, turning their frames of reference inside-out and upside-down to gain new insights.

Simplifying Complexity: Unitive Transformers tailor their communication to match their audience's capacity for understanding, breaking down complex ideas without losing their core essence.

Experiencing No-Self: Through their journey of questioning identity, they reach a state where they embrace the possibility of infinite identities but no fixed self-identity, signifying the complete dissolution of the ego.

Living What Is: They accept reality as it is, fully engaging with the ever-changing flow of life's moment-to-moment experiences and embracing the human condition in its raw form.

Converging Meditative and Living States: Unitive Transformers blend states of meditation with everyday activities, erasing distinctions between the mundane and the sublime.

Holding Up the Mirror: They reflect on and articulate the underlying processes of meaning-making, both for themselves and for others, enhancing collective understanding.

Transcending Personal Practices: Their mere presence can uplift and transform, drawing inspiration and teaching from all interactions and experiences.

Integrating Heart and Head: Unitive Transformers engage with life through both cognitive and emotional lenses, appreciating its fragility, wonder, fluidity, and inherent absurdities.

Listening Deeply: They excel in authentically reframing what they hear, valuing silence and pauses. Such listening enriches their interactions and deepens their connections with others.

In the realm of Unitive Potential, these attributes are not labeled as strengths or weaknesses but are seen as natural expressions of being. Unitive Transformers perceive everything "as is" without the need to assign evaluative attributes, embodying a holistic and integrated view of life.

Transformation to Unitive

The transition from an Integral to a Unitive Transformer is one of the most profound and gradual transformations you will experience. This journey doesn't follow a single path or process; it demands a deeper exploration of personal growth, societal impact, and cultural understanding.

Imagine moving from scuba diving in clear, sunlit waters to plunging into the murky depths where light barely penetrates. It's similar to rocketing into space, where you leave behind the comforting blue of Earth for the dark vastness of the cosmos. As you distance yourself from Earth, you begin to see things from a new perspective, grasping the relativity of what once seemed absolute from a ground-level view.

Here's a deeper look at what characterizes the Unitive transformation:

Commitment to Meaning: Engage deeply with self-actualization, striving to become a fully autonomous individual.

Contextualization: Place your purpose and vision within the broader context of your culture, lifetime, and multigenerational impact.

Communal Engagement: Connect with others who are similarly dedicated to deeply considered meanings and purposes in life. Engage in conversations that challenge deep-seated biases and assumptions.

Consideration of Time Frames: Reflect on your personal history, lifespan, and mortality and how they shape your daily actions and long-term aspirations.

Surrender to Emergent Order: Let go of the individual self to embrace a collective order, responding to a higher calling and universal values.

The Bottom Line

Transforming to a Unitive state is a path less traveled, requiring boundless patience and resilience through setbacks or regressions to earlier Potentials. Unitive Potential offers a profound new understanding of life's meaning and a direction that, while clear, remains open to continual discovery.

As we conclude our exploration of the seven Potentials, the next step is to apply this framework to teams and organizations. This ensures that transformative insights extend beyond individual growth and are shared and amplified across broader contexts.

PART 4

COLLECTIVE POTENTIAL

CHAPTER 10.

AUGMENT TEAM POTENTIAL

Peter Senge, MIT professor and author of *The Fifth Discipline*, once said, "It is amazing how often you come across teams with an average intelligence of over 120, but the team functions at a collective intelligence of about 60." This quote both bothered and inspired me. How is it possible that 'A players' become ineffective when they come together? What individual differences limit the capacity of the collective?

The simple yet uncomfortable answer is Potential.

Teams primarily operating at Domain and Vision-Centric Potentials often display collective intelligence surprisingly lower than their individual abilities would suggest. This occurs because, while the members are intelligent individually, they lack the synergistic interaction that amplifies their collective effectiveness. Thus, the team's collective intelligence might be around 60, even though the average individual IQ is over 120.

Conversely, teams where members operate at the Expansive and Integral Transformer Potentials can achieve collective intelligence far exceeding their individual capabilities, sometimes reaching 180 or more. This increase is because Transformer Potentials foster deeper collaboration and capitalize on diverse perspectives.

However, the effectiveness of mixed-Potential teams—especially those with one or two Transformer Potentials—depends heavily on the power dynamics within the team. For instance, if a Centric Potential leader oversees a team that includes Transformer Potentials, the team's overall effectiveness can be diminished. Centric leaders tend to exert power unilaterally, which often marginalizes the contributions of Transformer members, resulting in a collective Potential that is less than the sum of its parts.

I observed this dynamic within a senior leadership team where the Vision-Centric CEO led a mix of Domain-Centric and Vision-Centric executives, along with two Expansive Transformers. Despite the presence of the Transformers, the team's performance didn't improve because their contributions were overshadowed by the leadership style that favored earlier Potentials. This scenario perfectly illustrated a team where, unfortunately, the whole was less than the sum of its parts.

What Makes a Team Team

A few weeks ago, I asked a Group Vice President about the size of her team, and she responded, "eighty people." Can you spot the issue? Different people have varying definitions of what constitutes a team. Some refer only to their direct reports, while others might include their extended team or even the entire organization.

A true team is a small group of leaders who share a common purpose and rely on each other to achieve it. From my experience, the most effective teams consist of five to eight leaders.

Interdependencies increase complexity. Therefore, the larger the team, the more challenging it becomes to align members around shared objectives. This complexity is especially pronounced in senior teams, where leaders at the top are high achievers, independent thinkers, and highly ambitious—qualities that can sometimes lead to overdrive. They must balance their dependence on each other to achieve shared goals with the autonomy needed for their specific roles. This tension between alignment and autonomy is a core leadership challenge.

Most leadership teams have not yet evolved to Transformer Potentials, which would enable them to effectively balance both autonomy and alignment. Instead, many operate at the Centric Potential, prioritizing autonomy over alignment. Achieving alignment demands more collaboration, interaction, and capacity. It involves deep inquiry, deep listening, and trustful confrontations—tasks far more challenging than simply maintaining autonomy.

When a senior leadership team prioritizes autonomy over alignment, this behavior cascades down the organization, fostering a culture of silos. This misalignment often starts unconsciously at the top and permeates throughout the organization.

Siloed Leadership Team Story

A senior leadership team I coached faced a significant challenge: a siloed culture throughout the organization. Departments such as engineering, product, and customer success operated independently, collaborating minimally and mostly reacting rather than initiating. This placed the burden of innovation solely on senior leadership, who in turn blamed the rest of the organization for the lack of initiatives. However, the root of the problem lay at the top.

During growth discussions, the focus was almost exclusively on the head of sales. Other executives neither challenged the head of sales nor actively contributed new growth initiatives. Similarly, when the head of operations raised efficiency challenges, the other executives did not engage. They worked in silos within their team, defaulting every topic to the head of the relevant function and failing to collaborate in a cohesive and strategic manner.

When questioned about their lack of engagement in the growth conversation, the executives cited their trust in the heads of functions as domain experts. This mindset created silos at the top, which then permeated throughout the organization. By deferring every issue to the relevant function, they missed the opportunity to leverage collective cross-functional intelligence.

The team operated at the Domain-Centric Potential, allowing experts to dominate discussions without the level of challenge and collaboration expected at the Transformer Potential. This lack of confrontation and cooperation at the top perpetuated a siloed culture across the entire organization.

What Is Your First Team?

You can easily spot a siloed team by asking each member about their team. Without exception, everyone starts talking about the function they lead rather than the cross-functional team they belong to. This tendency underscores why aligning leadership teams at Domain and Vision-Centric Potentials is so challenging. These leaders view the business through their specific functional lens rather than adopting the broader, systemic perspective utilized by Expansive and Integral Transformers.

CEOs, ideally, should have a wider perspective since they don't have a functional lens. However, this is not always the case. If CEOs have evolved into Expansive or Integral Transformers, they are likely to have a more inclusive and comprehensive view of the business environment. Conversely, if CEOs stay within their Centric Potential, they will likely continue to depend on the familiar business perspectives they know best—whether that's finance, sales, marketing, or another domain.

Team Collective Potential

The Collective Transformer Potential greatly enhances a team's capacity for effective collaboration across various functions. In teams functioning at this level, traditional functional boundaries dissolve, and every member embraces a CEO-like mindset.

In Chapter Three, I highlighted that Potential drives performance, supported by a study correlating Potential with performance. Since teams are the fundamental building blocks of organizations, enhancing their Potential has a compounding effect on organizational performance and business results.

Currently, there is no scientifically validated tool to measure a team's collective Potential. However, an experienced Potential development coach can provide an evaluation. With the insights from this chapter, you'll also be equipped to assess your team's Potential effectively.

A crucial concept to grasp is that teams are distinct entities from their individual members. They function like organisms that encompass the team members but differ from them in significant ways. Team culture is a collective behavior that represents the team's Potential.

Senior leadership teams I have coached were predominantly Vision-Centric, while second-tier leadership teams were mostly Domain-Centric, with few Group-Centric teams. None were at the Expansive or Integral levels when we began working together.

The good news is that because team culture is a collective behavior, we can use the same iceberg framework, which we used to transform individual

Potential to boost a team's Potential. This involves deciding on the One Big Shift, identifying counter behaviors, connecting to the fears that drive these behaviors, constructing restraining assumptions, releasing confining safeguards, and pairing beliefs with interdependent beliefs.

Isn't it exciting? Transformation becomes much more manageable when we apply the same approach both individually and collectively.

Concurrent Transformation

Individual team members transform faster when their team transforms, and the team transforms faster when its members transform. They are interdependent. Consequently, companies that focus exclusively on either executive coaching or team coaching miss the essence of development. Individual and team growth are deeply interconnected, and prioritizing one over the other significantly slows down overall progress.

Development is most effective when pursued together. While you can work on your Potential individually, the social dynamics of team development drive motivation and accelerate progress. Team members hold each other accountable for both individual and collective development commitments.

Additionally, developing the team's Potential aligns individual members with the team's purpose, vision, values, and strategies. As the team evolves, members become adept at spotting hidden polarities, invisible blind spots, and deep-seated issues in real-time business actions. They learn to engage in meaningful conversations that help each other challenge and change outdated assumptions, safeguards, and beliefs.

Evolving Potential as a team is not only effective but also the fastest route to achieving rapid transformation.

Working In and On the Team

Ask any senior leader about their team meetings, and you'll likely hear the same story: dull, agenda-driven meetings focused on executing strategic decisions and reviewing performance. These meetings are examples of when the team works 'in the team.' Occasionally, teams hold offsite sessions to improve teamwork—this is when they work 'on the team.'

Rarely do teams integrate working 'in the team' with working 'on the team.' Yet, this integration is the secret sauce for evolving a team's Potential. Team members do so by calling 'timeouts' when conversations go off track. They pause to reflect on how they are collaborating and hold each other accountable not just for business outcomes but also for their developmental commitments.

Teams that haven't integrated working 'in' and 'on' the team may see some progress during coaching sessions and offsite meetings; however, they'll likely revert to old behaviors in business meetings. This indicates that the team has yet to reach its Transformer Potential.

Identify Your Team Potential

Team levels of Potential are similar to individual Potentials, reflecting specific thought and action patterns shaped by a dominant Potential within the team. The same twenty questions you used to identify your individual Potential in Chapter Three can be adapted to assess your team's Potential. Simply replace "I" with "we" in the questions and consider five distinct responses.

Why five? Because teams and organizations don't exhibit Self-Centric or Unitive Transformer Potentials. Teams and organizations function within five Potentials: Group, Domain, Vision, Expansive, and Integral.

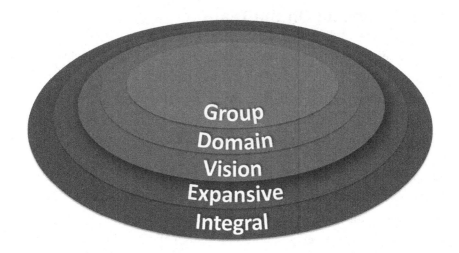

Figure 10.1 – Team Potentials

Like the Potentials of individuals, collective Potentials also encompass earlier Potentials, which remain fully accessible. This allows an Integral team the flexibility to operate at any of the earlier Potentials as needed while earlier Potentials are constrained by their own levels. These earlier stages are limited by their narrower leadership capacity, often leading to less effective performance.

To further identify your team's Potential, consider these four additional questions:

How do we make decisions?

Group-Centric: We follow the leader's decisions conservatively.

Domain-Centric: We rely on experts for decisions.

Vision-Centric: We decide through influence and compromise.

Expansive Transformer: We decide by consensus, incorporating diverse input.

Integral Transformer: We decide interdependently, considering long-term impacts.

How do we 'resolve' conflict?

Group-Centric: We avoid conflict or resolve it autocratically.

Domain-Centric: We resolve conflicts by defaulting to expert-winning solutions.

Vision-Centric: We negotiate conflicts for common objectives.

Expansive Transformer: We leverage conflicts to generate multiple solutions.

Integral Transformer: We transform conflicts into collective learning and innovation.

How do we give feedback?

Group-Centric: We avoid feedback to maintain face-saving.

Domain-Centric: We limit feedback to task performance.

Vision-Centric: We give feedback on key performance indicators.

Expansive Transformer: We engage in regular, candid, and mutual feedback.

Integral Transformer: We seek feedback to disrupt the status quo in and out of the organization.

How do we take risks?

Group-Centric: We dismiss ideas that risk our team unity and count on people with power and authority take risks.

Domain-Centric: We assess and mitigate risk using technical analysis and probability models.

Vision-Centric: We take bold, calculated risks to achieve audacious goals.

Expansive Transformer: We take risks to innovate and drive paradigm shifts.

Integral Transformer: We take risks to achieve our purpose and shape the world.

If your answers to the questions were inconsistent, you're not alone. Unlike individuals, teams rarely fit neatly into a single Potential category. It's uncommon to find a team that is purely Group or Domain-Centric, and even rarer to find one that operates entirely at the Expansive or Integral Transformer level.

In practice, most second-tier leadership teams, which are typically functional teams, tend to operate at the Domain-Centric level while aspiring to become Vision-Centric. There are exceptions, such as middle management teams in established organizations, where long-standing relationships may lead to some Group-Centric patterns.

Senior leadership teams, on the other hand, are more often Vision-Centric and aim to evolve into Expansive or Integral Transformers.

Therefore, we focus on two key team transformations: from Group/Domain-Centric to Vision-Centric and from Vision-Centric to Expansive/Integral Transformer. By targeting these transformations, teams can effectively elevate their collective Potential and drive meaningful organizational progress.

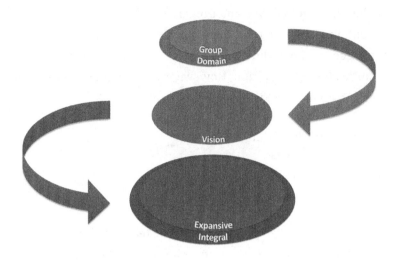

Figure 10.2 – Team Potential Transformations

Transforming from Group/Domain to Vision-Centric

Earlier in this chapter, we explored the challenges of a siloed leadership team—a common problem in teams that operate at the Group/Domain-Centric Potentials. In a Group-Centric environment, an "us vs. them" mentality prevails, often manifesting in conflicts such as those between finance and sales over budget allocation or between marketing and sales over customer acquisition strategies.

Domain-Centric Potential can lead to divisions even within the same function. For example, I once worked with a company where the marketing department was deeply divided between performance marketing and branding marketing. These two teams were constantly at odds over resources. The branding team argued that the short-term focus of performance marketing didn't contribute to long-term growth, while the performance marketing team claimed that branding was a waste of resources due to its unclear return on investment.

As this illustrates, both Group and Domain-Centric teams fall into the same siloed mentality. They focus on their specific functions, outputs, efficiency, and the need to be right, leading to fragmented efforts and missed opportunities for collaboration. However, these attributes must evolve as the team transitions to a Vision-Centric Potential:

- Function → Business
- Outputs → Outcomes
- Efficiency → Effectiveness
- Being right → Winning together

Let's explore how the Group/Domain-Centric team used the iceberg transformation model to make this shift to Vision-Centric Potential.

Deciding on the Team's One Big Shift

The most obvious difference between Group/Domain-Centric and Vision-Centric teams is that Group/Domain team members primarily advocate, while Vision-Centric teams primarily inquire. The siloed team mentioned earlier committed to adopting a new Vision-Centric behavior: asking questions to clarify all points of view and collaborating on shared goals they created together.

Identify Counter Behaviors

When the team inventoried behaviors that worked against their Vision-Centric goal, they identified the following:

- Advocating from their prioritized functional (and personal) agendas
- Driving narrow-focus, short-term initiatives
- Prioritizing their functional expertise
- Trying to be the best

- Relying solely on their data and distrusting other teams' data
- Opposing ideas to stand out
- Protecting their teams instead of the whole organization

Let's explore the underlying fears driving these behaviors, which impede the transition to Vision-Centric Potential.

Connect to Team's Fears that Drive Counter Behaviors

The key to addressing collective fear lies in recognizing that Group/Domain-Centric Potentials are rooted in dependency, while Vision-Centric Potential is grounded in independence. Dependency is driven by the need for external approval and validation, whether from the domain experts or authority figures, such as the board of directors.

Not good enough: Group/Domain-Centric teams, like individuals, fear that asking questions will prevent them from proving their competence. They choose advocacy over inquiry, worried that others won't recognize their expertise and mastery.

Losing control: They fear losing control of the narrative by asking questions, equating being out of control with chaos.

Being wrong: They fear being wrong and thus avoid conversations that might take them into unknown territory.

Damage relationships: They are worry of damaging relationships with key stakeholders.

These collective fears mirror those of individuals.

Construct Teams Restraining Assumptions

Breaking silos invites resistance fueled by fears based on assumptions, such as:

- "If we negotiate or inquire about other perspectives, we'll lose control."
- "If we collaborate and ask other stakeholders questions, our team will be seen as not good enough."
- "If we explore other perspectives, we might find something wrong."

To overturn these assumptions, teams start with small, safe experiments of the new behaviors and observe reactions.

Release Confining Safeguards

Safety within the team: Group/Domain-Centric teams feel safer interacting within their team than with other stakeholders.

Guarded with other stakeholders: They remain guarded with other stakeholders, displaying stiffness and reluctance through body language.

Dependence on knowledge and data: They heavily rely on knowledge and data, missing the information and wisdom beyond these confines.

Pair Beliefs with Interdependent Beliefs

In conversations with Group/Domain-Centric teams, a common belief often emerges: achieving results requires securing 'buy-in.' Consequently, asking questions and listening are not top priorities. Transformation begins when a siloed team experiments with both advocacy and inquiry— by actively asking questions and listening deeply.

Another critical shift is moving from focusing solely on outputs to emphasizing outcomes, from efficiency to effectiveness, and from just getting things done to creating real impact. This evolution involves embracing new polarities:

- Contribution AND impact
- Issue AND outcome

For example, rather than saying, "We need to increase inventory because it's below average," a Vision-Centric team would say, "We need to increase inventory so that we can fulfill the sales pipeline." The phrase "so that" connects each action to its intended impact.

Additionally, there's a subtle but significant shift from merely doing to embodying a state of being. A highly effective Vision-Centric team is not only aware of its state of being but can also clearly articulate it to explain their actions. This awareness of 'being' enhances their effectiveness in 'doing'.

Transforming from Vision-Centric to Expansive/ Integral Transformer

After coaching the siloed leadership team mentioned earlier for 18 months, the members successfully dissolved the silos within their ranks. Issues related to finance were no longer seen as solely the CFO's responsibility, and sales challenges were no longer just the CRO's problem. Instead, these became shared concerns, and the team approached them as a unified entity.

The team collaborated across all functions to tackle both profitability and growth challenges. Their efforts led to greater cohesion, and a subsequent 360-degree assessment with stakeholders showed a remarkable improvement in their collective leadership effectiveness, which surged from the 40th to the 80th percentile. This marked their successful transformation from Group/Domain-Centric to Vision-Centric.

However, this internal focus also revealed a new vulnerability. The team had become overly inward-looking and lacked a comprehensive understanding of the rapidly changing, complex market. As they worked on evolving to Expansive/Integral Potential, they recognized that they had not yet achieved this higher level collectively. This realization prompted another 18 months of transformation.

While the shift to Vision-Centric represents a move from dependence to independence, the transition to Expansive/Integral Potential involves moving from independence to inter-dependence. In this state, each team member remains independent but also relies deeply on the other independent members.

This transformation involves multiple shifts:

- Controlling → Letting go
- Certainty → Curiosity
- Having answers → Making sense
- Framing → Reframing
- Vision → Purpose
- Truth → Multiple truths

Let's explore how the team used the iceberg model to transform into an Integral Transformer team.

Decide on the Team's One Big Shift

Integral teams excel at:

- **Observing and acting simultaneously:** They are adept at both noticing and responding to emerging situations.
- **Inquiring and noticing:** They constantly ask questions and look for patterns in conversations.
- **Zooming in and out:** They quickly move from big-picture thinking to detailed analysis and vice versa.
- **Showing systemic curiosity:** They shift conversations with customers and business partners from transactional to relational, seeking to understand the broader ecosystem and the needs of their stakeholders' stakeholders.

- **Innovating for impact:** They focus on industry and world impact as success criteria beyond just the financial bottom line.
- **Facilitating the process:** In complex environments, they focus more on the process than on controlling outcomes.
- **Sensemaking:** Their collaboration evolves from merely hearing all voices to building on each other's understanding to create shared meaning.

The team's one Big Shift was "We are committed to engage with our primary stakeholders with deep listening and systemic awareness."

Identify Counter Behaviors

While deciding on new Expansive/Integral Transformer behaviors, the team identified Vision-Centric behaviors that were counterproductive:

Struggling with Uncertainty: The team grappled with a low tolerance for uncertainty and ambiguity, always seeking certainty, clarity, and control in their decision-making processes.

Neglecting Broader Goals: They had not extended their focus beyond the immediate company to consider the broader system, including stakeholders and their extended networks. For instance, while they maximized profits and increased efficiencies, they overlooked the side effects, such as burnout, on themselves, their families, and their teams.

Misalignment on Purpose: Although they aligned on business goals, they did not fully integrate their individual, team, and organizational purposes, nor did they explore how these purposes interconnect.

Connect to Team's Fears that Drive Counter Behaviors

The key fears driving counterproductive behaviors included:

Failing to Achieve Goals: At first, the fear of failure paralyzed the team as they transitioned toward Expansive Potential. The CEO, uneasy with challenging long-held habits of controlling outcomes, temporarily reverted to Vision-Centric behaviors.

Misalignment: They feared that considering multiple perspectives would prevent them from agreeing on a single direction.

Indecisiveness: They worried that balancing inquiry with advocacy would lead to slow or no decision-making.

Construct Teams Restraining Assumptions

The team identified assumptions linking their new Expansive/Integral Transformer behaviors to their fears:

- "If we inquire, we will be indecisive."
- "If we prioritize the wider system, we will fail to achieve our goals."
- "If we align for purpose, we will be misaligned about our business direction."

Release Teams Confining Safeguards

The team's false safeguard was their belief that delivering top and bottom lines was enough to ensure their safety—essentially, that their sole job was to control outcomes. This belief led them to focus heavily on controlling every aspect.

The biggest challenges emerged during board meetings. Initially, I avoided visiting their office two weeks before these meetings because the stress was so high. Team members were intensely focused on polishing their presentations to control outcomes.

Then, as the team was preparing to take calculated 'safe' risks and experiment with their assumptions and safeguards, COVID-19 hit. This unforeseen and massive 'experiment' accelerated their transformation.

In the first year of COVID, their business plummeted by 80%. They lost control of all anticipated outcomes, laid off and furloughed employees, and cut salaries and bonuses. Despite these drastic measures, they never paused their Potential development program.

I was astonished. They reduced their management team but kept me on. I was so surprised that I halved my fees for a year. Over the next 18 months, the team continued to develop, evolve and ultimately transformed into an Expansive/Integral Transformer Potential.

Pair Teams Beliefs with Interdependent Beliefs

Teams can develop the interdependent pole of many polarities. Here are a few examples where the team I coached initially leaned too much toward the left pole and gradually shifted to leverage both:

Outcome AND Process: Initially, the team's meeting agendas were solely focused on business performance and comparing results to objectives. Over time, these agendas became more flexible, allowing the team to work 'on the team' as much as 'in the team.'

Internal AND External: The team reduced their time spent in the board-room. After COVID-19 restrictions eased, they began meeting with customers and business partners together, integrating both internal and external insights.

Business Development AND People Development: The most striking shift was their consistent, determined prioritization of people development alongside business development.

I vividly recall a coaching session where we focused on purpose, vision, and thematic goals. When I asked them to suggest a thematic goal, all of them wrote an objective related to people development. Not a single executive suggested a business objective—that's a given.

Team Transformation Moves

From a development perspective, team transformation is complex and lengthy. Transformation doesn't happen overnight; it requires a strong commitment from team members. Here are a few highly effective transformation strategies.

Team Purpose

Most teams lack clarity about their purpose. Leadership teams sometimes mistakenly believe that the company's purpose is their own. This isn't the case. Teams must discover their purpose through conversations with their stakeholders, focusing on what stakeholders need from them.

During these conversations or surveys, conflicts of purpose may arise. The team must then work together to find common ground amidst these differences. A shared team purpose serves as the glue that fosters the alignment essential for a highly effective team.

Effective Team Meetings

Leaders often complain about wasting time in team meetings. Two main reasons contribute to boring and ineffective meetings: team members avoid conflict, or they face conflicts they can't resolve. As a result, team leaders often resort to unilateral decisions.

Teams that avoid conflict typically exhibit Group-Centric Potential. In these teams, leaders should actively seek out disagreements and encourage quieter members to share their perspectives, as diverse viewpoints can be very beneficial.

Teams that struggle to resolve conflicts tend to have a Domain-Centric culture. To address this, align the team around a specific purpose for an external stakeholder. When members focus on their individual functional perspectives, conflicts are hard to resolve. Shifting the focus to an external purpose helps to overcome this challenge.

Collective Build

Leadership teams often rush from one agenda item to the next, missing opportunities for generative dialogues. In generative dialogues, one person's idea serves as a starting point for others to build upon, rather than shifting to their own ideas. This collaborative process allows the team to become greater than the sum of its parts.

The collective build process starts with prompt or starter questions in the context of vision, values, strategies, goals, and objectives. For example:

- "Our most important objective for the quarter is..."
- "If we don't accomplish ____, we have failed."

Each member contributes one point. Then, the team leader facilitates a generative dialogue, starting with the less-heard people's ideas and moving to the most-heard at the end. Unlike brainstorming, where ideas are quickly tossed around, this approach involves the team working collaboratively on each idea as if it's the only one. Everyone contributes their best to refine, improve, and finalize it as a possible solution before moving on to the next idea.

Though this process might seem cumbersome at first, it becomes more efficient as the team integrates inputs from earlier suggestions. By the end, the number of ideas narrows down to a few that can be either integrated or voted on.

360° Stakeholders Team Assessment

Some teams struggle to identify their primary stakeholders. For instance, a leadership team at a medical technology company debated whether their main stakeholders were insurers, hospitals, surgeons, patients, investors, or employees.

This seemingly straightforward question can have a profound impact on the team's purpose, vision, strategy, and objectives. When the team eventually agreed that surgeons were their primary stakeholders, they achieved full alignment. However, many team assessments only reflect the team's internal perspective rather than a broader, systemic viewpoint.

A systemic assessment of the team's performance, relationships, and learning from all stakeholders provides valuable information that accelerates transformation, especially when the assessment differentiates feedback from primary and non-primary stakeholders.

Team Coaching

Team coaching is an action-inquiry process in which a coach helps the team enhance their collective performance, improve collaboration, and engage stakeholders to drive broader business transformation. A team coach can significantly accelerate this process by identifying the team's collective Potential, pinpointing key areas for change, and addressing counter behaviors, fears, assumptions, safeguards, and beliefs.

Team coaching serves as a powerful accelerator for both individual and collective Potential growth. This coaching occurs in dedicated sessions and through interventions during regular business meetings.

The Bottom Line

Augmenting Potential as a team is the fastest and most effective way to enhance performance, especially when guided by a Potential developmental coach. The framework used for individual growth can also be applied to teams as long as both individual and collective transformations occur simultaneously.

Leadership teams are only as strong as the member with the earliest Potential, particularly if that person is the CEO. The team itself is the best environment for boosting both individual and collective Potential.

With this in mind, let's explore how we can elevate the Potential of not just one team but the entire organization.

CHAPTER 11.

CREATE ORGANIZATIONAL GROWTH CULTURE

Teams are the building blocks of organizations. I define an organization as a team of teams. Therefore, organizational development is similar to team development and leadership development. If we agree on this, it becomes clear that the same Potential development framework applies to leaders, teams, and organizations alike.

Since most teams operate at Group, Domain, and Vision-Centric Potentials, the entire organization usually reflects these Potentials. In hierarchical organizations, the lower you go, the more functional and Group/Domain-Centric the operations become. As a result, many organizations develop a Domain-Centric or mixed Domain/Group-Centric culture.

On one hand, this expert-driven culture excels at building infrastructure, engineering airplanes, and curing diseases. On the other hand, it often results in people spending a lot of time and energy covering up weaknesses and engaging in politics.

Now, imagine the impact if an organization's culture could rise just one level to become Vision-Centric. Elevating organizational Potential in this way can increase profitability, improve employee retention, reduce operational mistakes, and enhance communication, delegation, and accountability.

The good news is that increasing organizational Potential follows the same process as boosting individual and team Potential. The levels of Potential and the iceberg transformation frameworks are the same. It's just common sense.

The Organizational Ripple Effect

Organizational Development professionals often make a critical mistake: they focus all growth efforts on up-and-coming leaders, middle management, high Potentials, and second-tier leaders. Rarely do the CEO and the executive team engage in their own personal and collective transformation of Potential.

This oversight is the primary reason why, despite billions of dollars spent on leadership development, the results tend to be minimal.

The key to growing organizational Potential is to begin with the top leadership then extend those efforts to second-tier leaders, creating a ripple effect throughout the organization. While starting at the top might seem daunting, especially if none of the senior executives are Expansive or Integral Transformer leaders, it's the most effective approach. When the CEO and the executive team lead by example, the organizational Potential moves through the path of least resistance.

The top-down ripple effect of growing organizational Potential works well for the same reason it's effective within teams: people grow faster because together we get better. By starting with the top leadership, we set the tone and build a culture that encourages growth at every level of the organization.

The Tech Company's Potential Growth

Returning to the tech company leadership team from the last chapter, they started as a siloed team operating at the Group/Domain-Centric Potential. Over 18 months, they transformed into a Vision-Centric team. When they reached the Expansive/Integral Transformer Potential, something remarkable happened: the senior leadership team made people their primary focus, alongside business growth.

This shift marked their transition into the Transformer zone, as they began to focus on more than just the financial bottom line. Employees were no longer simply a means to an end; they became the end goal themselves.

The senior team then invited second-tier leaders to join them on the same journey they had undertaken over the past two years. At the conclusion of an offsite where we launched a one-year Potential development program, the executive team of five gathered in a closing circle, sharing their experiences in a deeply emotional, tear-inducing conversation.

Over the following year, as I worked with both the senior and extended leadership teams, I witnessed the ripple effect of Potential growth spreading throughout the organization. Leaders developed a new language, quadrupled cross-functional collaboration, dismantled long-standing silos, and created an environment where people actively supported each other's Potential growth. Attrition levels dropped to unprecedented lows.

Most importantly, employees started to behave like human beings rather than cogs in a machine. They stopped shielding themselves and began experiencing a sense of fulfillment, meaning, and growth. They overcame imposter syndrome and emerged from hiding.

This transformation wasn't unique to this tech company. Every company I worked with that started at the top and extended to the second tier and beyond saw similar results. By following the science of Potential development and scaling these concepts, hundreds and thousands of people transcended behaviors, fears, assumptions, safeguards, and beliefs that had previously limited their capacity.

When people crack the Potential code, they create new practices that didn't exist before, overcoming the limits of traditional leadership development methods. This leads to a culture that self-augments Potential, moving beyond sporadic, exclusive, short-term interventions.

Organizations themselves don't change—individuals do. These individuals then invite their teams and organizations to change with them. However, organizations serve as powerful incubators for growing Potential, possessing a superpower called culture, which employees tend to adapt to—whether positive or negative.

A Potential development culture has the power to transform its members through symbiotic relationships. Leaders reshape the culture into one that fosters the growth of Potential, and this culture, in turn, becomes an incubator for individual growth of Potential. It's the perfect ecosystem for growth.

Potential Growth Culture

The common thread among all the companies I worked with to develop their Potential was the CEOs' genuine commitment to their own growth, as well as the growth of their leadership team and the entire organization. Supporting the personal development of employees wasn't just a line on their website—it was central to their purpose.

Employee growth was a priority. Imagine working with managers and colleagues who consistently check in on your progress toward your One Big Shift. Picture your coworkers making your development goals their priority. This is what a Potential growth culture looks like.

A Potential growth culture embraces the simple yet rare practice of intentionally growing all employees' Potential. It is rooted in the belief that a business prospers only when its people do.

In this culture, human growth and business growth are seamlessly linked. Organizations that focus solely on business development while ignoring Potential development often struggle with performance. Interestingly, organizations that prioritize both business growth and their people's Potential tend to achieve better results than those that focus only on the business.

This holistic approach creates an environment where both individuals and the organization can truly thrive.

The Cultural Bungee

The concept of the cultural bungee explains why highly developed leaders often face challenges in organizations that haven't evolved to match the Potential of these leaders. When leaders advance to a greater Potential than their organization's culture, they may unintentionally pull back to the organization's level. This dynamic makes it hard for more evolved leaders to succeed in less evolved organizations and is a key reason why many leadership development programs that focus only on individuals fail—they don't evolve the organizational culture at the same time.

Different companies operate at different cultural levels:

- **Group-Centric:** "Fit in and don't rock the boat."
- **Domain-Centric:** "We count on the experts here."
- **Vision-Centric:** "It's about the outcomes we achieve together."

When leaders try to advance beyond their organization's prevailing culture, they often face strong resistance that pulls them back. While some leaders succeed in moving the organization forward, most become worn down, revert to the existing cultural norms, or leave the organization altogether. As a result, many organizations lose their most evolved leaders.

Most organizations operate from a Domain-Centric Potential. However, individual leaders may develop beyond this, reaching a Vision-Centric or even Expansive/Integral Potential. Organizations often invest in these leaders' development, recognizing the need for growth. Yet, the culture within the organization frequently pulls these leaders back to the earlier Domain-Centric level, undermining those development efforts.

This dynamic is at the heart of the cultural bungee. The more advanced leaders try to move forward, the more the organizational culture pulls them back to the level where most of its members operate. Leaders who try to help the organization navigate complexity often burn out, give in to the dominant cultural norms, or leave. Even though organizations urgently need leaders with Vision-Centric or Expansive/Integral Potentials, they struggle to retain and accommodate them.

By understanding how culture impacts organizational Potential, we can recognize and address the cultural bungee. This allows us to develop strategies to evolve both individual leaders and the organizational culture together. Doing so creates an environment where evolved leaders can thrive and guide their organizations through complexity and change.

Building Potential Developmental Culture
Start at the Top

Most attempts to change organizational culture fail because they don't begin with the CEO and executive team. Top leaders must model Potential growth and openly share their experiences with the entire organization. When leadership shows a genuine commitment to development, it sets a powerful example for everyone else to follow.

Make Potential Growth Evergreen

Many leadership development programs are short-term and fragmented—some training here, a bit of coaching there, an offsite for team development, etc. But growing from one Potential level to another takes time and consistent effort. Sporadic initiatives won't change the culture. To make organizational Potential growth ongoing, we need practices embedded in daily business operations, ensuring growth is continuous and ever-present.

Integrate with Business Strategy

Potential development becomes ingrained in culture when it's aligned with business strategy. For example, if a new strategy focuses on expanding product offerings into a new market segment, identify the behaviors needed for success in that segment and determine the Potential level best suited to achieve it.

Measure Impact

Culture is shaped by the consistent behaviors demonstrated across an organization. These behaviors align with any of the five core Potentials. By creating surveys, we can measure the organization's current Potential levels and track progress over time.

Practice Daily

Potential growth becomes part of the culture when everyone—from the CEO to frontline employees—talks about personal development in team meetings, group discussions, and one-on-one conversations. Regular dialogue and focus on growth weave these practices into the fabric of the organization.

Create a New Language

Potential growth involves a developmental language with terms like One Big Shift, behaviors, counter-behaviors, fears, assumptions, safeguards, beliefs, and polarities. Companies often create their own terminology to describe practices and norms, building a sense of community and integrating developmental practices into daily routines.

Reach Critical Mass

For cultural change to take hold, a critical mass of leaders must create a ripple effect throughout the organization. If only the top two tiers of leadership focus on growing their Potential, it won't be enough. Depth is essential, meaning the third, fourth, and even lower tiers must also be involved to ensure lasting cultural change.

Ask and Give Feedback All the Time

A Potential growth culture thrives on continuous feedback. Formal systems like 360-degree surveys, along with informal feedback in all meetings, are crucial. Creating accountability circles where peers regularly give and receive feedback also strengthens this culture.

Role Model Potential Growth

Senior leaders play a key role in cultural transformation by openly discussing their own struggles with Potential growth. Change occurs when the core mindsets underlying behaviors are addressed. Leaders' stories of their personal development journeys inspire others, demonstrating that they are not alone in their growth.

Establish Egalitarian Culture

Although hierarchical structures remain, titles should not dictate the ability to give or receive feedback. Everyone should be able to engage in feedback, regardless of their position. Meritocracy fosters new ideas, while hierarchy can stifle them. Growth in Potential should be a focus for everyone, including the CEO.

Develop a Coaching Culture

While a Potential development coach can accelerate growth in individuals and teams, this approach isn't scalable across an entire organization. The goal is to create a coaching culture among top leaders, who then foster a peer coaching culture within other tiers, generating a ripple effect of growth.

Create Reflections Practice

Reflection is crucial for growth. Without time dedicated to reflecting on behaviors, fears, assumptions, safeguards, and beliefs, meaningful change is unlikely. Teams should also reflect on their collective performance. Public reflections, such as fishbowl practices—where cross-functional groups reflect on challenges while observed by others—are powerful tools for fostering cultural growth.

During fishbowl reflective practices, cross-functional groups form an inner circle to reflect on an event, failure, or challenge they are facing. An outer circle of observers watches and provides feedback to the inner circle. Such public reflections are highly effective in building a Potential growth culture.

Like the principle that neurons that fire together wire together—learning becomes working, and working becomes learning. Therefore, collective reflections are vital for developing a high Potential culture.

Form Communities of Potential Growth

An organization with a Potential growth culture operates as a community of developmental communities—whether they are intact teams, cross-functional groups, or teams of teams. These communities value their members as individuals seeking growth rather than just as positions with job descriptions, roles, and responsibilities.

People are most motivated by the opportunity to grow. When we embed this drive into the organization's operations, it becomes a powerful force for change throughout the organization.

It's not enough to simply get the right people on the bus. We also need to focus on the growth of all the people already on the bus. Potential growth serves as an alternative to the war for talent. This approach not only supports individual development but also cultivates a culture where collective growth fuels organizational success.

Articulate Developmental Principles

Instead of relying on slogans, mottos, and other platitudes that are often forgotten unless revisited on the company website, organizations that cultivate a Potential growth culture establish deeply held principles that guide daily decisions. These principles are rooted in a fundamental belief in the power of individual growth. They serve as the foundation for actions and behaviors, ensuring that the commitment to development is woven into the fabric of the organization and reflected in every decision and interaction.

Bridgewater Associates' Potential Growth Culture

Bridgewater Associates, the largest hedge fund in the world with over $235 billion in assets under management, attributes much of its success to its growth culture, a principle championed by its founder, Ray Dalio. Since its founding in 1975, Dalio has emphasized the importance of creating meaningful work and relationships through rigorous and thoughtful inquiry.

Dalio aimed to establish a meritocracy within the firm, leading him to develop a set of principles that form the backbone of Bridgewater's management philosophy. Chief among these principles are radical truth and radical transparency—encouraging open and honest dialogue to allow the best ideas to emerge and prevail.

In his book *Principles*, Dalio elaborates on the growth culture he envisioned: "At most companies, everybody works two jobs: their actual job and the extra job of managing other people's impressions of them to make themselves look good. In such an environment, people tend to hide their mistakes, and those of others, out of fear that pointing them out will lead to their own mistakes being exposed."

Bridgewater's commitment to these principles has been recognized, with the firm being named a Great Place to Work, with 95% of its employees voting for that certification. Additionally, it was ranked as a Top Workplace, coming in as the second largest employer in Connecticut.

Bridgewater's example shows how deeply held principles of Potential growth can drive organizational success and create a culture where meaningful work and open inquiry are central.

The Bottom Line

Creating a Potential growth culture involves simultaneously developing the Potential of individuals and teams at scale. The most effective way to transform a culture is by starting with the CEO and executive team then expanding to the second and third leadership tiers to build a critical mass of Transformers. This approach creates a ripple effect of Potential growth throughout the organization.

Companies that cultivate a growth culture view people's development as an end in itself, not just a means to achieve business growth. These companies often reach high levels of success, which can be linked to their culture. When leadership teams evolve into Transformer Potentials, they understand that developing people as a standalone goal is crucial for fostering a Potential growth culture.

During business challenges, many companies cut expenses, lay off employees, and halt leadership development efforts. However, companies committed to a growth culture continue investing in development even in tough times. This ongoing commitment ensures that Potential is nurtured, regardless of business performance.

Business results are a lagging indicator, while Potential growth is a leading indicator. By prioritizing Potential growth, organizations can build a resilient and adaptable culture that drives sustained success.

CHAPTER 12.

PUTTING IT ALL TOGETHER

"I am who I am," Brian confidently said to me a few years ago, drawing authority from his role as CEO. "Brian being Brian," his executives would say, rolling their eyes and nodding, convinced that neither he nor they were likely to change at this point.

They soon discovered that this belief was a myth. People don't experience our personality; they experience our Potential. When we elevate our Potential from one level to the next, people experience us differently, making it seem as if our personality has changed. But it's not just about how others perceive us—our own experience of life transforms as we grow our Potential.

The journey through seven levels of Potential represents seven different life paths. We can stop at any one of the earlier stations or continue the journey to the final destination, where we live a meaningful, fulfilling, abundant, and love-filled life, making a lasting impact on our loved ones, teams, organizations, and society.

This book serves as a comprehensive guide to expanding your Potential to its fullest capacity, enabling you to align with others more effectively, even in unpredictable situations or amid strong resistance. Transforming your Potential is a straightforward yet powerful framework. By identifying your current level of Potential and following the 5-step 'iceberg' process, you can transform yourself, your team, and your organization.

As we conclude, let's summarize some key concepts that will help you put it all together.

Key Concepts

Potential is expansive: Unlike other developmental models that describe growth as a vertical progression, this framework views development as expanding our Potential into a broader space of capacity, consciousness, and complexity. This expansive approach enables richer, more comprehensive growth, equipping us to navigate life's complexities with greater resilience and effectiveness.

We operate across multiple levels of Potential: While I've referred to people by their level of Potential (such as Integral, etc.), we aren't confined to a single level. We operate across multiple levels, with our default level representing our Center of Gravity. This Center of Gravity shows our primary mode of operation, but we also have access to all previous levels of Potential. We can intentionally choose to engage at these earlier stages or, under pressure, revert to them unintentionally. This fluidity allows for ongoing adaptation and growth, utilizing the strengths of each level of Potential when needed.

Transformer Potentials enable superior effectiveness in hyper complexity: The openness to consider multiple perspectives, values, visions, and strategic options helps Expansive, Integral, and Unitive Transformers excel in navigating rapidly changing circumstances. By continuously questioning their assumptions, biases, and beliefs, these Transformer Potentials are highly effective in dynamic, multifaceted situations.

240

From outside-in to inside-out: Self, Group, and Domain-Centric individuals define themselves based on external validation—what others think of them. In contrast, Vision-Centric individuals and Transformers build their identity around their internal 'north star.' This inner compass guides their decisions and actions, helping them stay aligned with their core values regardless of external pressures. This shift from relying on outside-in validation to being guided from the inside-out fosters authenticity and resilience in managing life's complexities.

Greater Potential generates better performance: As individuals and teams elevate their Potential, they enhance their ability to lead, make decisions, and, ultimately, better business outcomes.

Potential is measurable: Tools like the Washington University Sentence Completion Test (WUSCT), subject-object interviews, and the self-assessment from Chapter 3 can measure Potential. These assessments should be taken every few years to track developmental progress. Regularly measuring Potential ensures that you stay on course and continue advancing effectively.

Idealizing the real world: The seven levels of Potential represent abstract concepts that can't fully capture the complexity of human experience. Human beings are more intricate than any single framework can convey, and there are many paths to growth. This framework serves as a developmental map to guide your growth journey, offering structure while recognizing the richness and complexity of real life.

The inner game drives the outer game: To change our external actions (doing), we must first transform our internal world (thinking and feeling). Our behaviors and outcomes are deeply shaped by our thoughts and emotions. By shifting our inner game, we can have a more powerful and lasting impact on our outer game, leading to more meaningful growth and improved performance.

Boosting Potential is like upgrading our operating system: New behaviors are like new apps—they require a compatible operating system to function smoothly. These behaviors won't work effectively if our internal system—made up of our fears, assumptions, safeguards, and beliefs—is outdated. Boosting Potential involves upgrading this internal operating system, allowing new behaviors to be successfully integrated and sustained over time.

No transformation without integration: Integrating our earlier Potentials into our current Potential is essential for growth. It means consolidating all previous levels and staying deeply connected to each so you can instantly recognize when you revert to an earlier level—whether intentionally or unintentionally.

The strengths of the current Potential (Center of Gravity) are the weaknesses of the next Potential (Growth Edge): Transformation requires letting go of the strengths you rely on at your Center of Gravity and embracing the new strengths of your Growth Edge.

The Transformation Framework

Our transformation framework, which spans the six transitions between the seven levels of Potential, is based on the iceberg model. Here's a breakdown of the key steps:

Decide on the One Big Shift

This is the mother of all changes that you adopt from your growth edge Potential. The shift should be:

- Adaptive
- About you
- Affirmative

- Observable
- Life-changing
- Not about the outcome

Identify the Counter Behaviors

Recognize behaviors that undermine your One Big Shift—what you are doing and not doing that counteracts your growth.

Connect to the Fears that Drive Counter Behaviors

Identify what worries, scares, or stresses you about doing the opposite of these counter behaviors.

Construct Restraining Assumptions

Develop assumptions as "if...then" narratives:

- The 'if' part describes the new growth edge behaviors (or opposites of the counter behaviors).
- The 'then' part outlines the consequences of the fears associated with these behaviors.

Release Confining Safeguards

Let go of the major safeguards that our subconscious uses to protect us:

- **Identity and Self-worth:** Controlling outcomes, intellectual criticism, and relationship-pleasing tendencies.
- **Footholds:** Fixed ideas that we hold onto.
- **Equals:** Different ideas we use interchangeably without noticing.
- **Rules:** The 'shoulds,' 'musts,' and 'woulds' that the little voice in our head tells us.

Pair Beliefs with Interdependent Beliefs

As we progress through the levels of Potential, we shift from seeing single beliefs and values to understanding them as interdependent pairs, known as polarities. The more we leverage both poles equally, the more our Potential grows.

Let's recap the transformation framework for each one of the six Potential transformations.

Decide on the One Big Shift

We select the One Big Shift from the behaviors of the next level of Potential - our Growth Edge. The One Big Shift zeroes in on one of these behaviors, driving the transformation forward. Below is a guide to how the One Big Shift changes along the six transformations:

From Self to Group-Centric

- **Community glue:** Strengthening connections within the group.
- **Following norms:** Adhering to group standards and practices.
- **Loyal to the group:** Prioritizing group needs and interests.
- **Respecting tradition:** Valuing and upholding established practices.
- **Trusting authority:** Relying on leaders and accepted structures.

From Group to Domain-Centric

- **Challenging authority:** Questioning when there is a misalignment with what you know.
- **Taking a stand on professional issues:** Providing data to support your position.

- **Expressing openly what you want and need:** Being clear and assertive.
- **Showing your unique personality and voice:** Based on expertise and knowledge.
- **Winning arguments by being "right:"** Demonstrating mastery and knowledge.
- **Contributing to the group with professional mastery:** Sharing expertise.

From Domain to Vision-Centric

- **Focusing on outcomes over process:** Replacing efficiency with effectiveness.
- **Collaborating across the organization:** Working with interdisciplinary teams and leaders with different viewpoints.
- **Speaking directly at issues:** Addressing problems openly, even in risky situations.
- **Giving and asking for direct feedback:** Being straightforward and honest.
- **Replacing statements with questions:** Inquiring as much as advocating.
- **Facilitating conversations:** Guiding discussions rather than controlling them.
- **Getting things done through others:** Delegating effectively.
- **Allocating time for reflection:** Observing oneself from the outside.

From Vision-Centric to Expansive Transformer

- **Shifting focus from self to others:** Observing and sharing insights.
- **Pausing to observe:** Reflecting on what's happening within oneself and others during conversations.
- **Inviting challenging and opposing views:** Welcoming different perspectives.

- **Questioning purpose, vision, values, strategies, and processes:** Reflecting on core principles.
- **Challenging existing norms:** Replacing stable culture with creative and collaborative practices.
- **Listening deeply:** Reframing the meaning of the conversation partner.

From Expansive to Integral Transformer

- **Integrating Vision-Centric power with Expansive insights:** Combining strengths.
- **Collaborating with loose agendas:** Co-creating visions and strategies with others.
- **Being tuned, present, and attentive:** Reframing how others make sense of their experiences.
- **Integrating opposing views and beliefs:** Aligning decisions.
- **Exposing blind spots:** Encouraging others to reveal yours.
- **Encouraging conflict:** Surfacing differences in values and perspectives.
- **Giving and receiving transformational feedback:** Going beyond incremental improvements to underlying values, beliefs, emotions, assumptions, and narratives.

By deciding on the One Big Shift and focusing on these transformative behaviors, you can effectively move from your Center of Gravity to your Growth Edge.

Identify Counter Behaviors

Developing into your next level of Potential requires identifying the counter behaviors linked to your Center of Gravity. These counter behaviors work against your Growth Edge and must be addressed to enable successful transformation. Here are the counter behaviors most typical to each one of the Centers of Gravity.

Self-Centric

- Manipulating others
- Forcing my way
- Winning at all costs
- Protecting my turf (it's mine)
- Taking credit for others' efforts
- Bragging about myself and exposing other people's weaknesses
- Getting angry quickly and losing my temper
- Blaming others

Group-Centric

- Avoiding conflict
- Holding back creative expression
- Expressing disagreement only behind the back (passive-aggressive)
- Playing by the rules
- Acting to fit in
- Submitting my agenda to others' agendas
- Waiting for approvals to take actions
- Not speaking when disagreeing
- Not initiating changes
- Not making decisions if not sure of management position
- Not advocating opinions
- Not setting goals

Domain-Centric

- Arguing endlessly about my position
- Jumping to solve problems without paying attention to what people are experiencing
- Insisting on doing things my way

- Getting too much into the weeds and stuck in the details
- Criticizing other people's work
- Defending my position furiously
- Attempting to 'winning' debates and arguments
- Counting solely on data to prove my points
- Expecting others to show a similar commitment to professionalism as I do
- Operating independently because it's more efficient
- Not accepting 'good enough' work unless it's perfect
- Not admitting my mistakes and shortcomings
- Not expressing emotions and feelings
- Not asking for help when I'm stuck
- Not accepting feedback and getting defensive
- Not delegating when too much is at stake
- Not listening well to other people's points of view

Vision-Centric

- Seeking credit (more than sharing credit)
- Talking too much in meetings
- Working too hard to get buy-in rather than inquiring
- Driving myself and others excessively hard to get results
- Compromising long-term sustainability
- Defending from unwanted intrusions to the vision
- Brushing off perspectives that don't support the vision
- Getting carried away with too many ideas and goals
- Neglecting the details or over-preferring the big picture
- Neglecting personal needs and relationships
- Compartmentalizing issues without connecting their inter-dependencies.
- Missing the parts that make the whole
- Not evaluating my assumptions
- Directing everyone and everything to control the results

Expansive Transformer

- Losing outcome orientation
- Not aligning with peers and managers due to individualism
- Slow decision-making due to attempting to reach a consensus
- Initiating too many ideas without enough delegation

By identifying these counter behaviors, you can understand what actions are holding you back and identify the fears that drive these behaviors.

Connect to Fears that Drive Counter Behaviors

Fears are the distressing and troubling emotions we feel when trying new Growth Edge behaviors or when acting opposite to the counter behaviors. Here is a summary of the fears that drive counter behaviors for each level of Potential:

Self-Centric

- Staying out of trouble
- Losing the game
- Surviving
- Not getting caught
- Being eliminated
- Being dominated
- Being blamed

Group-Centric

- Being rejected
- Being avoided or ignored
- Being deserted or abandoned

- Being excluded, expelled, cast out, or exiled
- Losing the relationship
- Being seen as non-collaborative, unfriendly, or non-supportive

Domain-Centric

- Being undistinguished
- Being wrong
- Being unprofessional
- Being not as good as the others
- Being seen as weak
- Not being good enough
- Having no answers
- Making mistakes
- Being inefficient
- Failing to execute
- Not performing up to expectations
- Being blamed for others' mistakes

Vision-Centric

- Being dependent
- Losing control
- Being just one among many
- Not meeting standards or goals
- Being cast in a stereotype
- Not accomplishing
- Not learning
- Failing to execute
- Missing deadlines and milestones
- Being incompetent
- Miss opportunities

- Slowing down
- Being interrupted/disrupted
- Being overwhelmed

Expansive Transformer

- Being trapped in a rigid environment
- Being sucked back into an earlier Centric Potential
- Being biased
- Not being in the flow
- Being disoriented
- Missing part of the picture
- Being overwhelmed by complexity
- Being unaware of dependencies
- Being the problem
- Being misinformed
- Discriminating others
- Solving the wrong problem

By identifying these fears, we can understand what emotions drive our counter behaviors and find the assumptions our subconscious mind makes to protect us.

Overturning Restraining Assumptions

Assumptions are narratives crafted by the subconscious mind to shield us from the fears, anxieties, and probable consequences of those fears—essentially, to protect us from worst-case scenarios. Connecting behavior to fear creates an assumption constructed as 'if [behavior], then [fear].' Here are typical assumptions for each one of the Potentials.

Self-Centric

- If I tell the truth, I'll be eliminated
- If I follow orders, I'll lose
- If I take care of others, they'll eliminate me
- If I collaborate with others, I won't survive
- If I'll address other people's needs, they'll dominate me
- If I'm honest, they will use it against me
- If I do what they want, they will blame me
- If I work with them, they will use me

Group-Centric

- If I challenge my manager, they will hold grudges against me
- If I take a stand, they will reject me
- If I say directly what I need, they will ignore me
- If I demonstrate my unique personality, I won't be part of the team anymore
- If I win the argument and am "right," I'll lose the relationship
- If I stand out by demonstrating virtuosity, they will exclude me in the future

Domain-Centric

- If I'm undistinguished, I'll lose my seat at the table
- If I don't argue my position, I'll be proven wrong
- If I don't jump to solve the problem, somebody else will solve it
- If I don't insist on doing things my way, I'm undistinguished
- If I'm not in the details, I'll be seen as unprofessional
- If I admit mistakes, I'm not good enough
- If I delegate, I'll fail to execute
- If I ask for help, I'll be seen as weak

- If I accept feedback, I'm not as good as the others
- If I show emotions, I'm unprofessional

Vision-Centric

- If I ask too many questions, I'll be disrupted
- If I listen too much to others, we won't accomplish anything
- If I try to integrate other perspectives, I'll lose control
- If I don't get buy-in, we won't execute
- If I try to connect the dots, we will lose precious time and miss opportunities and deadlines
- If I'm hands-off, I'll become dependent on others
- If I don't solve all the problems, I'm incompetent

Expansive Transformer

- If I make fast decisions, I will miss part of the picture
- If I focus on outcomes, I will be stuck at Vision-Centric Potential
- If I don't question others, I'll be unaware of the dependencies
- If I don't question myself, I'll be biased
- If I don't initiate many ideas, I'll be stuck in the rigid system
- If I don't ask for everyone's opinion, I will be misinformed
- If I don't leverage individualism, I'll lose my freedom of choice

These assumptions help us understand the self-protecting safeguards our subconscious minds created for us.

Release Confining Safeguards

Safeguards are subconscious commitments we create to shield ourselves from our fears, but they often end up hindering our growth. Here's a breakdown of the safeguards at each level of Potential:

Self-Centric

Identity:

- I'm my wants and needs
- I'm successful if what I wish happens
- I do whatever works for me

Self-worth:

- I'm worthy when I get what I want

Footholds:

- It's me against everybody else
- Everybody cares only about themselves
- Are you with me or against me?
- It's them or me
- I win or lose
- It's my way or no way

Equals:

- Success is material things
- Power is money
- Loss is collateral damage.

Rules:

- Rules are created to break them
- Rules are created to find loopholes
- Rules can be broken as long as I don't get caught

Group-Centric

Identity:

- I'm my relationship, group, religion, or caste
- I'm a proud member of...
- I'm nobody outside my group
- I'm liked, loved, and accepted

Self-worth:

- I belong to this company, group, team
- I'm a member of this club

Footholds:

- Us vs. them
- They don't belong with us
- Our truth is the only truth
- Our group is superior
- I wanted to protect my reputation
- I shouldn't have done that
- We're like family, and I take pride in being part of it
- Loyalty means everything
- Blood is thicker than water
- We are stronger together

Equals:

- Meeting expectations = success
- Complying with my manager = safety
- We win = I win
- I am = What others think of me

- Loyalty = respecting our tradition
- Hierarchy, status, money = better
- Right way = diplomatic way
- Criticism = they don't like me
- Feedback = personal disapproval

Rules:

- I should
- I shouldn't
- I must
- I always
- I never

Domain-Centric

Identity:

- I'm my profession ("I'm a doctor")
- I'm an expert (I'm a surgeon")
- I'm special (I'm an ex-Googler)

Self-worth:

- I'm worthy when I win an argument, when I'm right, and when the other is wrong
- I'm worthy when I'm perfect, when I stand out, and when I'm the best
- I'm worthy when my way becomes everyone's way
- I'm worthy when I'm in control
- I'm worthy when I solve problems and fix bugs
- I'm worthy when others come to ask my advice

Footholds:

- Knowledge is power - the more I know, the more powerful I am
- Never being seen as less than competent
- Never being not in control of facts
- Never lose status
- Never be seen as vulnerable or weak
- Always be certain and have the right answer
- Not knowing or making mistakes is unacceptable
- If things don't go according to the plan, find who and what's responsible
- Get the best practices and standards right

Equals:

- Knowledge = Trust
- Feedback = criticism = not good enough
- Effective = Efficient
- Truth = Data
- Performance = Expertise

Rules:

- Follow procedures and gather data
- If you don't know something, learn it
- Do things the right way—"good enough" isn't sufficient
- Best practice is the safest option
- Exceptions are risky
- Tangibles are prioritized over intangibles
- "Evidence is necessary"

Vision-Centric

Identity:

- I'm the master of my destiny
- I'm my success
- I'm results-oriented (I'm my results)
- I'm whatever I want to be
- I'm an achiever
- I'm a high performer (I'm my performance)
- I'm conscientious
- I'm a fast mover
- I'm decisive
- I'm effective
- I'm independent

Self-worth:

- My self-worth depends on how much my board, peers, and team buy into my vision.
- I feel worthy when people support my strategies.
- I'm less worthy if I don't deliver the expected results or when I'm indecisive.

Footholds:

- Linear sequential planning and avoiding non-linear
- Analytical thinking
- Neglecting biases and assumptions
- Juggling many balls
- Agreeing to disagree, Leaving personal views aside.
- Focusing on positives rather than on problems
- Never-ending commitment
- Making it all happen

- Finding the root cause and predicting the future

Equals:

- Success = results, performance, and outcomes
- Prediction = future
- Solving problems = generating solutions
- Optimization = effectiveness
- Choices = independence
- Prioritization = decision making
- Advocating = changing others' minds
- Complexity = contradictions = inconsistencies = contingencies
- Feedback = growth. Mistakes = opportunities to learn.

Rules:

- Thinking out of the box
- It's all about the results
- Change is the only constant
- Backed by science, framework, or a model
- We need to be rational
- Getting things done
- Matter of fact

Expansive Transformer

Identity:

- I build my identity on values, uniqueness, or truth

Self-worth:

- I generate my self-worth from my capacity to contextualize.

Footholds:

- I can never be objective.
- If everything is relative, how do I know when something doesn't depend on something else?

Equals:

- Better = egalitarian
- Context = meaning
- Complexity = progress
- Uniqueness = independence

Rules:

- The inner game runs the outer game.
- There is no right answer
- I'm not one thing
- What you get isn't what you see
- If you think you're in control, you aren't

By recognizing and releasing these confining safeguards, you can remove the barriers that inhibit growth and pave the way for transformation.

Pair Beliefs with Interdependent Beliefs

Beliefs come in opposing pairs, known as polarities. When we hold strongly one belief, unable to see and leverage the interdependent pair, we are stuck in our Center of Gravity. The over relying values are on the left, and the neglected values are on the right. We transform to our Growth Edge when we leverage both poles. Here are the pairs of beliefs for each level of Potential:

Self-Centric

- Urgency AND Patience
- Skeptical AND Trust
- My wants AND Other people's wants
- Protect myself AND Protect others
- Survive AND Thrive

Group-Centric

- Pleasing others AND Expressing myself
- Generalizing AND Exceptualizing
- Idealizing AND 'Real'izing
- Tactful AND Candid
- Meeting others' expectations AND Setting my own expectations
- Loyal AND Objective
- Following norms AND Questioning norms
- Dependent AND Independent
- Positive AND Authentic
- Status AND Merit
- Conforming AND Questioning

Domain-Centric

- Tangible AND Intangible
- Quantitative data AND Qualitative data
- Doing things right AND Doing the right things
- Efficiency AND Effectiveness
- Advocating AND Inquiring
- Directing AND Collaborating
- Being right AND Being aligned
- Details AND Big Picture
- Perfecting AND Delivering

Vision-Centric

- Goal AND Experience
- Outcome AND Process
- Change the world AND Change myself
- Predicting AND Sensing
- Controlling AND Letting go (of outcomes)
- Open to feedback AND Accept feedback
- Doing AND Being
- Future AND Present
- Science AND Art
- Analytical AND Intuitive
- Achieving AND Questioning

Expansive Transformer

- Relative AND Absolute
- People (oriented) AND Action/task (oriented)
- Now AND Future
- Inquiring AND Integrating
- Learning AND Transforming
- Negotiable AND Non-Negotiable
- Consensus AND Decisiveness
- Adaptive AND Firm
- Process AND Outcome

By recognizing and leveraging these interdependent beliefs, you can leverage both of them to grow your Potential effectively. When you leverage both poles, you are harnessing the upsides of both poles and avoiding the downsides of them, facilitating a more comprehensive and adaptive transformation.

Transformation Moves

There are three common transformation moves for all Potentials. The first is growing our awareness about how we operate in the world through a reflective practice that enables us to observe ourselves from an external perspective, as if from a balcony. The second is the practice of inquiry—asking ourselves questions about our behaviors, fears, assumptions, safeguards, and beliefs. The third is the practice of seeking feedback from others about our behaviors.

In addition to these common moves, there are specific moves to each Potential level:

Self to Group-Centric

Create incentives for collaboration: Condition success on teamwork.

Group to Domain-Centric

Ask questions: What am I noticing (seeing, hearing)? What am I feeling about what I'm noticing (emotions, sensations)? What's important to me (my need/value)? Did I get it right? Would you be willing to...?

Domain to Vision-Centric

Expansiveness: Acquire new knowledge and experience through collaboration with adjacent domains and cross-functional leaders from different disciplines.

Find Your Why: Articulate a powerful purpose statement that forms the core for setting a vision, following the two-part formula of *contribution* and *impact*.

Clarify Your Vision: Develop a short-term manifestation of the purpose that generates energy for you, your team, and your organization.

Establish Your Values: Choose three values that you are willing to pay the price to uphold and share them with your team, family, and beyond.

Convert statements into questions: Reframe what you want to say as questions to inquire.

Ask for feedback: Consistently seek feedback from those around you.

Reflect Consistently: Allocate time daily to step back and observe yourself in action. Follow a cycle of reflecting, planning, acting, and observing.

Build Trust with Deep Listening: Share observations as inquiries about what others feel and what's at stake for them.

Vision-Centric to Expansive Transformer

Reflection Practice: Establish daily reflection times about how you are doing, feeling, and thinking.

Leverage Both Outcomes and Processes: Make the *process* an *outcome* so that the *outcome* becomes a *process*.

Systemic Awareness: Make the team you belong to your 'first team' rather than the team you lead.

Practice Inquiry: Convert statements into questions and observations into hypotheses.

Build Trust with Deep Listening: Reframe to others what you notice about how they feel, what's at stake for them, and how they make sense of situations as a check-in question.

Test Your Assumptions: Test assumptions in small-scale, safe situations to observe how others respond and how you act, think, and feel.

Develop 4-D Thinking: Identify primary stakeholders, step into their perspectives, engage the entire team in systemic stakeholder relationships, prioritize relationship-building over selling, balance inquiry with advocacy, shift interactions from transactional to relational, and collect data on stakeholders' perspectives for a comprehensive view.

Expansive to Integral Transformer

Develop 5-D Thinking: Envisioning long-term impacts through Future-Backward thinking, reflect on pivotal past experiences with Past-Forward thinking, role-play competitors to uncover blind spots as Villain Stakeholders, identify overlooked or invisible stakeholders to broaden focus, and explore how external systems like political and environmental factors affect strategic decisions.

Real-Time Reflection: Reflect continuously in a loop where action feeds reflection and reflection feeds action.

Develop Body Intelligence (BQ): In addition to IQ and EQ (emotional intelligence), develop deep awareness of your body and listen to what it tells you in different situations.

Expansive to Unitive Transformer

The transition from Integral to Unitive Transformer is the longest and slowest. Unlike earlier transformations, this shift lacks a single, defined path or process. It involves taking the Integral transformation deeper into ourselves, others, cultures, and society:

Commit to a Meaningful Life: Create a meaningful life through self-actualization and becoming an autonomous person.

Contextualize Purpose and Vision: In the context of culture, lifetime, and multiple generations.

Commune with Like-Minded Individuals: Engage in insightful conversations to question inert biases and assumptions.

Consider Time Frames: Reflect on your history, lifetime, and mortality in daily and aspirational situations.

Surrender the Self: Favor emergent order, a higher calling, and overarching values.

Augment Team Potential

A team is a small group of leaders united by a common purpose who depend on each other to achieve their goals. While individual members work autonomously within their specific functions and roles, their independence often creates tension between their shared purpose and personal autonomy.

Most leadership teams function at a Centric Potential, where autonomy often takes precedence over alignment, resulting in siloed cultures within organizations. In contrast, teams operating at the Transformer Potential collaborate effectively across functions.

Teams serve as the ideal environment to enhance the Potential of their members both individually and collectively. As the team transforms, its members evolve more rapidly, and vice versa. Development is most effective and swift when it happens together, making team-based growth the fastest route to transformation.

The secret sauce of team transformation lies in integrating working 'in the team' with working 'on the team.' Your team can identify its Potential using the same twenty questions from Chapter Three, focusing on the relevant replies while eliminating the Self-Centric and Unitive Transformer replies, as these are irrelevant to teams.

Additional questions to help identify your team's Potential include:

- How do we make decisions?
- How do we resolve conflict?
- How do we give feedback?
- How do we take risks?

We focus on the two most relevant team transformations:

- From Group/Domain-Centric to Vision-Centric
- From Vision-Centric to Expansive/Integral Transformer.

If the essence of transforming to Vision-Centric is the shift from dependence to independence, the shift to Expansive and Integral is the shift from independence to interdependence.

Teams that transform from Group/Domain to Vision-Centric work on these shifts:

- Function → Business
- Outputs → Outcomes
- Efficiency → Effectiveness
- Being right → Winning together

Teams that transform from Vision-Centric to Expansive/Integral Transformer work on these shifts:

- Controlling → Letting go
- Certainty → Curiosity
- Having answers → Making sense
- Framing → Reframing
- Vision → Purpose
- Truth → Multiple truths

Let's summarize the two major team transformations through the 5-step iceberg framework.

Deciding on Team One Big Shift

Just as individuals decide on a new behavior for the next level Potential (Growth Edge), teams decide on a collective behavior to engage from the Growth Edge. For example:

Group/Domain to Vision-Centric

Asking questions to clarify all points of view and collaborate on shared goals they created together.

Vision-Centric to Expansive/Integral Transformer

Observing and acting, inquiring and noticing, zooming in and zooming out, showing systemic curiosity, innovating for impact, facilitating the process without controlling the outcomes, and making sense of their experiences.

Identify Team Counter Behaviors

Group/Domain to Vision-Centric

- Advocating from their prioritized functional (and personal) agendas
- Driving narrow-focus, short-term initiatives
- Prioritizing their functional expertise

Vision-Centric to Expansive/Integral Transformer

- Seeking certainty, clarity, and control

- Not prioritizing goals outside the immediate company
- Not aligning on purpose

Connect to Team's Fears that Drive Counter Behaviors

Group/Domain to Vision-Centric

- Not good enough
- Losing control
- Being wrong

Vision-Centric to Expansive/Integral Transformer

- Fail to achieve goals
- Misalignment
- Indecisiveness

Construct Teams Restraining Assumptions

Group/Domain to Vision-Centric

- If we negotiate or try to inquire about other perspectives, we'll lose control.
- If we collaborate and ask other stakeholders questions, our team will be seen as not good enough.
- If we explore other perspectives, we might find something wrong.

Vision-Centric to Expansive/Integral Transformer

- If we inquire, we will be indecisive.
- If we prioritize the wider system, we will fail to achieve our goals.
- If we align for purpose, we will be misaligned about our business direction.

Release Team's Confining Safeguards

Group/Domain to Vision-Centric

- Prefer to interact within the team rather than with other stakeholders.
- Stay closely guarded when interacting with other stakeholders.
- Depend heavily on knowledge and data, missing the information and wisdom outside knowledge and data.

Vision-Centric to Expansive/Integral Transformer

- As long as we deliver results, we are safe.
- The future of the company is in our hands.
- We have control of the outcomes.

Pair Beliefs with Interdependent Beliefs

Group/Domain to Vision-Centric

- Outputs AND Outcomes
- Advocacy AND Inquiry
- Efficiency AND Effectiveness
- Contribution AND Impact
- Issue AND Outcome

Vision-Centric to Expansive/Integral Transformer

- Outcome AND Process
- Internal AND External
- Business Development AND People Development

Major Team Transformation Moves

Here are five transformation moves we discussed lengthy in Chapter 10.

1. **Discover the Team's Purpose:** Through conversations with stakeholders.
2. **Facilitate Effective Meetings:** Dig for disagreements and align the team around an external stakeholder's shared purpose.
3. **Spend More Time in Generative Dialogue:** Use the collective build process, where one person's idea generates a starting point for others to develop further without shifting to their own ideas.
4. **Take a 360° Stakeholders Team Assessment:** Involve internal and external stakeholders.
5. **Engage a Potential Development Team Coach:** Use team coaching as an action-inquiry process to improve collective performance and stakeholder engagement.

By focusing on these key moves and transformations, teams can effectively enhance their collective Potential and create a more collaborative, innovative, and effective organizational culture.

Create an Organizational Growth Culture

Creating a culture of Potential growth involves developing the Potential of both individuals and teams simultaneously and on a large scale. The most effective way to transform a culture is to start with the CEO and the executive team. By extending this transformation to the second and third leadership tiers, you create a critical mass of transformers who will drive a ripple effect of Potential growth throughout the organization.

Companies that cultivate a growth culture understand that developing people is not just a means to achieve business growth but an end in itself.

These organizations are often highly successful, attributing their success to their growth-oriented culture. Leadership teams that evolve into the Transformer Potential recognize that prioritizing people development as a standalone goal is crucial for fostering a Potential growth culture.

In challenging times, many companies cut expenses, lay off employees, and suspend leadership development efforts. However, organizations committed to creating a growth culture continue to invest in their people, even during difficult periods. They understand that while business results are lagging indicators, Potential growth serves as a leading indicator.

The good news is that enhancing organizational Potential mirrors the process of boosting individual and team Potential. The levels of Potential and the iceberg transformation frameworks remain consistent across all levels. A culture focused on Potential development can transform its members through the symbiotic relationships within the organization. Leaders initiate this cultural change, turning the organization into an incubator for personal and professional growth and creating an ideal growth ecosystem.

Integrating human growth with business growth is essential for a Potential growth culture. Organizations that focus solely on business development while neglecting Potential development often struggle with performance. Conversely, organizations that prioritize both business and people development achieve better results than those that focus exclusively on business.

Building Potential Developmental Culture

1. **Start with the CEO and Executive Team**: Leadership must model their growth for the rest of the organization.
2. **Make Growth Efforts Ongoing and Never-Ending**: Consistent practices embedded in daily business routines are essential.

3. **Align Growth Efforts with Business Strategy**: Ensure that Potential development supports the company's strategic objectives.
4. **Measure Impact**: Use Potential development pulse surveys to assess progress and impact.
5. **Encourage Open Conversations:** All employees, from the CEO to entry-level staff, should engage in discussions about their Potential development during team, group, and one-on-one meetings.
6. **Create a New Language of Potential Development:** Introduce key concepts such as One Big Shift, behaviors, counter behaviors, fears, assumptions, safeguards, beliefs, and polarities into the organization's vocabulary.
7. **Reach Critical Mass of Transformative Leaders:** This will create a ripple effect across the organization.
8. **Formal and Informal Feedback:** Establish a culture of constant feedback.
9. **Be Open About Growth Struggles:** Leaders should share their challenges to inspire others.
10. **Egalitarian Approach to Potential Development:** Everyone, including the CEO, should participate in growth activities.
11. **Develop a Coaching Culture:** Senior leaders should coach their direct reports, which in turn coach their own direct reports, creating a cascade of growth.
12. **Establish Reflection Practices:** Incorporate reflection into daily routines across the organization.
13. **Form Communities of Potential Growth:** Develop communities within teams and teams of teams to foster collective growth.

Creating a Potential growth culture integrates everything we do as individuals, teams, and organizations, making development an inherent part of our work rather than a separate activity. This approach ensures that Potential development is continuous and woven into the fabric of daily operations.

Putting it All Together

The Potential model is profound for several reasons.

First, Potential development integrates all aspects of individual, team, and organizational growth. Unlike sporadic and fragmented efforts such as leadership development programs, offsites, and executive coaching, it synchronizes the development of leaders, their teams, and the organization into a coordinated, cohesive process.

Second, Potential development becomes a fundamental part of our daily work rather than an isolated activity. People grow and learn on the job, evolving alongside their peers, bosses, and direct reports. This approach ensures that growth is continuous and woven into the fabric of daily operations.

Third, Potential development is evergreen. It is an ongoing process, not limited to specific events like coaching, training, or offsites. Instead, it is a living, breathing element of the organizational culture, always in motion and continuously evolving.

The Urgency of Growth

There has never been a more critical time in human history for us to grow together. The world is increasingly complex, unpredictable, and divided. Existential threats—from nuclear conflict to climate change—underscore the urgent need for continuous evolution, both individually and collectively. Our survival depends on it.

A New Way of Being

Potential growth offers a transformative way to understand ourselves and the world. It represents a new way of being human. Imagine a world where everyone evolves into Expansive, Integral, and Unitive Transformer Potentials. What possibilities would open up? How would life change for our children, grandchildren, great-grandchildren, and future generations?

The Power of Potential Growth

Potential growth can make this vision a reality. It is already happening. By joining this movement, you become part of a transformative force capable of changing the world. Time is precious, and life is short. Embrace the journey of Potential growth and make a lasting impact.

Map for Your Future

The end of our exploration into evolving our Potential is just the beginning of your journey. The Potential framework is a map with a defined destination, and you have a choice: grow or remain where you are. This map will guide you, helping you explore the infinite possibilities that Potential growth offers.

It's a calling. When you respond to this calling, your Potential growth story will rewrite your life story. I hope our paths will cross in the future so I can hear your story of transformation. Together, we can change the world, one Potential at a time.

APPENDIXES

Appendix A

Theoretical Foundations

My intention in writing this book was to provide a practical framework without delving deeply into the theoretical underpinnings of the Potential framework. However, the scientific basis of this book is profoundly rooted in decades of research by renowned developmental psychologists. These scholars have translated their theories into leadership practices, frameworks, and assessments.

Stage Development Theories

My work is primarily rooted in three development theories:

Robert Kegan's Order of Consciousness

Robert Kegan is a developmental psychologist, licensed therapist, organization development consultant, and former professor of Adult Learning and Professional Development at Harvard Graduate School of Education. He taught there for forty years before his retirement in 2016. Kegan also served as the Educational Chair for the Institute for Management and Leadership in Education and co-directed the Change Leadership Group.

Kegan's groundbreaking work on the stages of consciousness is detailed in two books:

- *The Evolving Self: Problem and Process in Human Development*, Harvard University Press, 1982
- *In Over Our Heads: The Mental Demands of Modern Life*, Harvard University Press, 1998

Susanne Cook-Greuter's Maturity Framework

Susanne Cook-Greuter developed the MAP instrument and its assessment methodology. As an international authority on adult development, she is the strategic advisor and research director at the Vertical Development Academy. Cook-Greuter is renowned for her seminal work in adult development theory and frequently speaks at international conferences. She has analyzed over 11,000 MAP tests across more than 200 academic and business contexts.

Her theoretical work provides the foundation for transformative leadership, integrating a developmental perspective into corporations and executive teams.

Her publications include:

- *Transcendence and Mature Thought in Adulthood*, Rowman & Littlefield Publishers, 1994
- *Creativity, Spirituality, and Transcendence: Paths to Integrity and Wisdom in the Mature Self*, Praeger, 1999
- *Postautonomous Ego Development: A Study of Its Nature and Measurement*, Integral Publishers, 2010

William Torebrt

Bill Torbert is Leadership Professor Emeritus at Boston College and serves on the Boards of the Amara Collaboration and Global Leadership Associates (home of the Global Leadership Profile). He holds both a B.A. and a Ph.D. from Yale and has developed a new paradigm of social science and social action called Collaborative Developmental Action Inquiry (CDAI).

His publications include:

- *Managing the Corporate Dream*, Dow Jones-Irwin, 1978 (Alpha Sigma Nu award winner)

- *The Power of Balance: Transforming Self, Society and Scientific Inquiry*, Sage, 1991 (Terry Award finalist)
- *Action Inquiry: The Secret of Timely and Transforming Leadership*, Berrett-Koehler, 2004
- *Seven Transformations of Leadership*, top ten Harvard Business Review leadership articles of all time (HBR, 2005)

Stage Development Assessments

The Seven Levels of Potential integrate three leadership assessments developed by the above scholars:

Subject-Object Interview (SOI)

The SOI is an interview-style assessment where a certified practitioner evaluates the level of consciousness based on Robert Kegan's adult development theory. This is detailed in *A Guide to the Subject-Object Interview: Its Administration and Interpretation* by Robert Kegan & Lisa Lahey, Minds at Work, 2011.

Global Leadership Profile (GLP)

The GLP is an assessment based on the Washington University Sentence Completion Test, further developed and provided by Global Leadership Associates. It measures the seven Action Logics as developed by Bill Torbert.

Maturity Profile (MAP)

The MAP assessment is based on the Washington University Sentence Completion Test, further developed through Dr. Susanne Cook-Greuter's extensive research at Harvard University and provided by the Vertical Development Academy.

Beena Sharma, president of the Vertical Development Academy, is a certified MAP scorer, a Master Coach in Leadership Maturity Coaching, and a lead facilitator in VeDA's coach certification program.

Stage Development Frameworks Comparison

For those familiar with or using any of the above theories or assessment tools, here is a conversion table of the theories to Potential Development:

Potential		Robert Kegan	Susanne Cook-Greuter	William Torbert
Self		Self-Sovereign	Self-Centric	Opportunist
Group	Centric	Socialized	Group Centric	Diplomat
Domain			Skill Centric	Expert
Vision		Self-Authored	Self-Determining	Achiever
Expansive			Self-Questioning	Redefining
Integral	Transformer	Self-Transforming	Self-Actualizing	Transforming
Unitive			Construct Aware	Alchemist
			Unitive	

Table 13.1 – Comparison of the Potential Framework with
Adult/Vertical Development Theories

Potential Transformation Framework

The Potential Transformation 'Iceberg Model' was developed based on my last seven years of intensive work with five developmental schools of thought.

Immunity to Change (ITC)

Developed by Robert Kegan and Lisa Lahey, the Immunity to Change framework has significantly influenced my work. I was a resident practitioner for a year at Minds at Work, working closely with Kegan and Lahey, as well as their faculty, including Deborah Helsing and Maria DeCarvalho. I eventually became certified as an Immunity to Change Coach. The ITC framework is thoroughly explained in the book *Immunity to Change: How to Overcome It and Unlock the Potential in Yourself and Your Organization* (Leadership for the Common Good), Harvard Business Review Press, 2009.

Maturity Coaching Intensive (MCI)

My work has also been profoundly influenced by the Vertical Development Academy (VeDA) program, Maturity Coaching Intensive, facilitated by Beena Sharma in collaboration with Susanne Cook-Greuter. This program, based on the MAP instrument, has been instrumental in adapting Polarity Management to the seven levels of Potential.

The Leadership Circle

In my practice, I use the Leadership Circle Profile (LCP) as a primary 360-degree assessment, individually and collectively. The LCP aligns with Robert Kegan's adult development theory, and extensive research was published by the Leadership Circle founders in two books:

- *Mastering Leadership: An Integrated Framework for Breakthrough Performance and Extraordinary Business Results*, Robert J. Anderson and William A. Adams, Wiley, 2015
- *Scaling Leadership: Building Organizational Capability and Capacity to Create Outcomes that Matter Most*, Robert J. Anderson and William A. Adams, Wiley, 2019

Growth Edge Coaching

I have deep gratitude for Jennifer Garvey Berger, with whom I worked for over a year in her three-part Growth Edge Coaching series: *Conversations at the Edge, Dancing at the Edge,* and *Mapping the Edge.* Jennifer Garvey Berger is a founding partner and CEO of Cultivating Leadership. She combines profound theoretical insights with practical methods to enhance leaders' lives. Jennifer holds a doctorate in adult development from Harvard University, where she studied and worked with Robert Kegan. Before focusing on translating powerful research into real-world applications, she was an Associate Professor at George Mason University. Her key books include:

- *Changing on the Job: Developing Leaders for a Complex World,* Stanford Business Books, 2011
- *Simple Habits for Complex Times: Powerful Practices for Leaders,* Stanford Business Books, 2015
- *Unlocking Leadership Mindtraps: How to Thrive in Complexity,* Stanford Briefs, 2019
- *Unleash Your Complexity Genius: Growing Your Inner Capacity to Lead,* Stanford Briefs, 2022

Polarity Management

The influential work of Barry Johnson, who developed the Polarity Management framework, has been instrumental in my approach. Some complex problems do not have straightforward solutions. Effective leaders must recognize and manage these types of issues. Polarity Management offers a distinctive model and set of principles that encourage leaders to view situations from new perspectives. The framework includes exercises to enhance skills and case studies to apply the model to seemingly unsolvable problems. Special thanks to Leslie DePol and Barry Johnson at Polarity

Partnership Inc. Barry's key book is *Polarity Management: Identifying and Managing Unsolvable Problems* (HRD Press, 2014).

Team and Organizational Potential Development

My work on team and organizational Potential development, described in Part 4 of the book, was influenced by:

Peter Hawkins

Peter Hawkins was my teacher, mentor, and coach throughout the three-year Systemic Team Coaching certification program he led. Peter is Professor of Leadership at Henley Business School, University of Reading, UK, and Emeritus Chairman of Bath Consultancy Group. He has helped organizations worldwide connect strategic change, organizational culture, and leadership development.

His key books include:

* *Leadership Team Coaching: Developing Collective Transformational Leadership*, 4th Edition, Kogan Page, 2021
* *Systemic Coaching: Delivering Value Beyond the Individual*, Routledge, 2019
* *Creating a Coaching Culture*, Open University Press, 2012

Global Leadership Associates (GLA)

My leadership philosophy underwent significant evolution during the year-long certification programs with Global Leadership Associates. Founded by Bill Torbert, Elaine Herdman Barker, and Richard Izard, GLA provided exceptional faculty, including Danny Morris, Kirsty Leishman, Nick Owen, and Trish Silber. My work has been deeply influenced by GLA's programs on Vertical Leadership Development, Action Inquiry, the Global Leadership Profile (GLP), Vertical Organizational Development, and the Advanced Practitioner Program.

Deliberately Developmental Organization and Immunity to Change

Returning to the work of Robert Kegan and Lisa Lahey, their major impact on my approach to team and organizational Potential development is rooted in their Immunity to Change framework, detailed in their book *Immunity to Change*. Their concept of a Deliberately Developmental Organization (DDO) is further explored in *An Everyone Culture: Becoming a Deliberately Developmental Organization* (Jossey-Bass, 2007).

Appendix B

Potential Development Program

A successful Potential development program integrates three critical components: Executive Coaching, Team Coaching, and Group Coaching.

Executive Coaching

Executive coaching is crucial to the success of a Potential development program. It is most effective when integrated and synchronized with team coaching. Coachees set coaching objectives that support both their individual development and team goals, sharing their commitments and receiving feedback from their teams and other stakeholders. This alignment ensures that individual and team goals are in harmony, maximizing the return on investment.

One-on-one sessions with certified Potential development coaches assist leaders in evolving from their Center of Gravity to their Growth Edge. The interdependence between executives and their teams means that the growth of one reinforces the growth of the other, making concurrent executive and team coaching essential.

Executive coaching helps leaders navigate conflicting perspectives, integrate opposing directions, and overcome limiting beliefs. This comprehensive approach not only enhances their professional effectiveness but also enriches their personal lives.

Team Coaching

Systemic team coaching is where real change occurs. This approach involves partnering with a team in a co-creative and reflective process, focusing on its dynamics and both internal and external relationships. The goal is to inspire the team to maximize its Potential and achieve common objectives.

Among various team development methods, systemic team coaching is the most complex, demanding, and effective. It equips teams to navigate the challenges of today's hyper-complex world, fostering collaboration across the organization and aligning team goals with broader objectives.

Integrating team coaching into regular business meetings enhances its effectiveness. In this approach, the coach observes staff meetings and intervenes in real time to encourage behaviors that improve the team's functionality both 'in the team' and 'on the team.' These real-time interventions ensure that developmental changes practiced in team coaching sessions are immediately applied and reinforced in real life.

Team coaching also helps teams gain clarity of purpose, explore and adhere to their values, and fully optimize their Potential, even in virtual environments. It embeds team-based thinking at every level of the organization, ensuring alignment and relevance during significant transitions.

Group Coaching

Group coaching is a scalable solution for leadership development. It gathers leaders from various functions or departments, helping to break down organizational silos. This approach is especially effective for middle management, as it promotes cross-functional collaboration and alignment.

Group coaching can be implemented within a single organization or across multiple organizations. Within an organization, it extends leadership development beyond the top teams, reaching into various departments or functions. When conducted across different organizations, it provides personal development opportunities for executives, encouraging peer learning and exchange.

Rolling Out a Potential Development Program

Implementing a Potential development program requires a strategic approach to ensure it achieves the desired impact across the organization. Key principles are outlined in Part 4 of the book:

Start at the Top: Engagement from senior leadership is crucial. Top leaders must model their own growth, showing commitment to the program and inspiring the rest of the organization. Their active participation helps embed the new developmental language and practices into the organizational culture.

Make Development Evergreen: Potential development is an ongoing, integral part of the organizational culture. Continuous coaching, woven into daily business practices, ensures long-term growth and development. Sporadic training sessions and workshops alone are insufficient for sustained transformation.

Reach Critical Mass: Achieving cultural change requires a critical mass of leaders to undergo Potential development. It's vital to expand the program beyond top leadership to include middle management and frontline leaders. A broad base of developed leaders will create a ripple effect, driving change throughout the organization.

Set Up Feedback Systems: Effective Potential development programs include robust feedback mechanisms. Regular 360-degree feedback, formal assessments, and informal feedback sessions are essential for leaders to understand their progress and identify areas for improvement.

Conclusion

Potential development programs offer a transformative approach to leadership and organizational growth. By enhancing the foundational capacities of individuals, teams, and entire organizations, these programs equip them to navigate the complexities of today's business environment more effectively. Through thoughtful design and strategic implementation, organizations can cultivate a culture of continuous growth, agility, and resilience.

As you begin this journey, remember that Potential Development is not a one-time effort but an ongoing, evolving process. Embrace it as a pathway to unlocking unprecedented levels of organizational success and growth.

Appendix C
About the Author

Dave Osh is a transformative catalyst dedicated to evolving leadership Potential to create a ripple effect of unity in our divided world. As the founder of Varlinx, he leads large-scale leadership transformation programs in global companies.

Over the past decade, Dave has collaborated with top developmental psychologists, integrating adult development theories into practical frameworks for transforming individuals, teams, organizations, and society.

Dave's diverse career includes roles as a management consultant, CFO, and COO of Nasdaq-listed companies, and CEO of the multinational company Qnet and the tech startup Execuvite. He has led multinational teams in 34 countries, working in Israel, Hong Kong, Malaysia, and Singapore. Since moving to the USA in 2016, Dave has coached executive teams to achieve significant outcomes in companies such as eBay, Netflix, Dolby, Intuit, Stripe, UKG, Alcon, Marvell Technology, and 10XGenomics.

A former fighter pilot and senior leader in the Israeli Air Force, Dave led hundreds of combat and reconnaissance missions in 20 years of service. He transitioned from a command-and-control style to leading with love, compassion, and oneness while still excelling in Volatile, Uncertain, Complex, and Ambiguous (VUCA) situations.

Dave is the author of *Outgrow Middle Management: Accelerate Your Climb to the Top* (Morgan James Publishing, 2014) and *CEO Potential: Transcend Self, Team, and Organization for Lasting Success in a Complex World*. He publishes the weekly newsletter "Potential Development" and hosts the CEOpeek show. He is an internationally sought-after speaker, including

TED. Dave lives in the San Francisco Bay Area, where he enjoys playing rock guitar, skiing, and hiking around the world.

You can connect and follow Dave on LinkedIn: https://www.linkedin.com/in/daveosh/

Appendix D
About Varlinx

Varlinx is a leadership and organizational development boutique firm founded in 2017 and registered in the State of California. Varlinx has developed cohesive, practical, and measurable programs designed to transform individuals, teams, organizations, and, perhaps, society.

Varlinx specializes in the development of C-suite executives. The firm's programs help leaders navigate the complexities of leadership transitions and integrate newly created executive roles into their organizations. Varlinx coaching services extend to individual and collective C-suite coaching, emphasizing leadership effectiveness as the primary performance indicator.

Varlinx coaching philosophy is built on five pillars:

1. **Leadership Effectiveness**

    Leadership effectiveness is at the core of Varlinx coaching approach, measured through the Leadership Circle Profile (LCP). Studies highlight the importance of leadership effectiveness, with the top 10% of leaders operating at the 80th percentile, compared to the bottom 10%, which perform at the 30th percentile. Varlinx recognizes that only 20% of leaders have evolved to the level required at the C-suite, and the firm works to bridge this gap.

2. **Transformational Shift**

    Varlinx helps clients identify the One Big Shift—a single, crucial behavior change that can make a transformative impact on the organization. This shift unlocks new capacities, boosting leadership effectiveness and business performance.

3. **Developmental Lens**

   Grounded in adult development theory and vertical development practice, Varlinx coaching emphasizes the continuous evolution of leadership along a measurable developmental continuum. Leaders are guided to understand their location on this continuum and are supported in setting strategic developmental goals, represented by their One Big Shift.

4. **Concurrent Coaching**

   Varlinx integrates individual leader coaching with team coaching through a synchronous, concurrent approach. Executives and their teams are treated as interdependent entities, with mutual growth shaping both individual and collective performance.

5. **Systemic Team Coaching**

   A key element of Varlinx coaching is systemic team coaching, where the team enhances its collective performance and leadership to engage more effectively with all stakeholders. This approach enables teams to navigate hyper-complex environments, align with larger organizational objectives, and embed team-based thinking throughout all levels of the organization. Systemic team coaching benefits include fostering a teaming culture, optimizing virtual teams, and providing tools for handling complex team dynamics.

Key Benefits of Varlinx Potential Development

- Enhances leadership effectiveness at the C-suite level
- Unlocks transformational shifts that elevate individual and team capacities
- Guides leaders through measurable stages of development using a developmental lens
- Strengthens team collaboration and systemic conflict resolution

- Prepares organizations for fast-paced, complex environments and change

With its expertise in handling complex team dynamics and leadership transitions, Varlinx continues to be a trusted partner in leadership development for executives and their organizations, ensuring sustained growth and transformation.

Learn more on Varlinx website: https://www.varlinx.com/

Made in United States
North Haven, CT
09 July 2025

70495636R00173